Alex Peltes
Feb 2002

P9-DEM-723

Also by Seth Godin

The Information Please Business Almanac
The Guerrilla Marketing Handbook (with Jay Levinson)
Permission Marketing

You can find this manifesto, along with slides and notes and other good stuff, at:
http://www.ideavirus.com.

UNLEASHING THE IDEAVIRUS
by SETH GODIN

With a Foreword by Malcolm Gladwell

**Stop marketing at people!
Turn your ideas into epidemics by helping
your customers do the marketing for you.**

HYPERION

NEW YORK

This book is dedicated to Alan Webber
and Jerry Colonna. Of course.

Do You Zoom, Inc.
145 Palisade Street
Dobbs Ferry, NY 10522

Copyright © 2001 Do You Zoom, Inc.
Ideavirus™ is a trademark of Do You Zoom, Inc. So is ideavirus.com™.

Designed by Red Maxwell

All right reserved. No part of this book may be used or reproduced in any man-
ner whatsoever without the written permission of the Publisher. Printed in the
United States of America. For information address: Hyperion, 77 W. 66ᵗʰ Street,
New York, New York 10023-6298.

Manufactured in the United States of America

              Library of Congress Cataloging-in-Publication Data
Godin, Seth.
    Unleashing the ideavirus / Seth Godin ; foreword by Malcolm Gladwell.—1st
ed.
      p. cm.
    Includes index.
    ISBN: 0-7868-8717-6
    1. Word-of-mouth advertising. 2. Marketing. I. Title

  HF5827.95 .G63 2001
  659.13'3—dc21

                                   2001024492

FIRST EDITION

10 9 8 7 6 5 4 3 2 1

SNEEZE HERE!

Here's what you can do to spread the word about *Unleashing the Ideavirus:*

1. Send a friend to www.ideavirus.com so they can download the free manifesto.
2. Visit www.fastcompany.com/ideavirus to read the *Fast Company* article.
3. Buy a copy of the hardcover book for a friend online.
4. Get a free copy for your Palm at www.peanutpress .com.

The #1 question people ask me after reading
Permission Marketing:

"So, how do we get attention to ask for permission in the
first place?"

This manifesto is the answer to that question.

CONTENTS

Contents

Contents

Contents

Contents

FOREWORD

The notion that an idea can become contagious, in precisely the same way that a virus does, is at once common-sensical and deeply counter-intuitive. It is common-sensical because all of us have seen it happen: all of us have had a hit song lodged in our heads, or run out to buy a book, or become infected with a particular idea without really knowing why. It is counter-intuitive, though, because it doesn't fit with the marketer's traditional vision of the world. Advertisers spent the better part of the 20th century trying to control and measure and manipulate the spread of information—to count the number of eyes and ears that they could reach with a single message. But this notion says that the most successful ideas are those that spread and grow because of the customer's relationship to other customers—not the marketer's to the customer.

For years, this contradiction lay unresolved at the heart of American marketing. No longer. Seth Godin has set out to apply our intuitive understanding of the contagious power of information—of what he so aptly calls the ideavirus—to the art of successful communication. *Unleashing the Ideavirus* is a book of powerful and practical advice for businesses.

But more than that, it is a subversive book. It says that the marketer is not—and ought not to be—at the center of successful marketing. *The customer should be.* Are you ready for that?

MALCOLM GLADWELL
Author of *The Tipping Point*
www.gladwell.com

INTRODUCTION

If you don't have time to read the whole book, here's what it says:

> Marketing by interrupting people isn't cost-effective anymore. You can't afford to seek out people and send them unwanted marketing messages, in large groups, and hope that some will send you money.

> Instead, the future belongs to marketers who establish a foundation and process where interested people can market to *each other*. Ignite consumer networks and then get out of the way and let them talk.

If you're looking for mindblowing new ideas, you won't find them in this, or any other marketing book. Guerrilla marketing, 1:1 marketing, permission marketing—these ideas are not really new, but they are thoughtful constructs that let you figure out how to do marketing better. The fact is, if we built factories as badly as we create advertising campaigns, the country would be in a shambles. This book will help you better understand the time-honored marketing tradition of the ideavirus, and help you launch your own.

Questions this book answers:

- Why is it foolish to launch a new business with millions of dollars in TV ads?
- Are the market leaders in every industry more vulnerable to sudden successes by the competition than ever before?
- Should book publishers issue the paperback edition of a book before the hardcover?
- What's the single most important asset a company can create—and what is the simple thing that can kill it?
- Every ad needs to do one of two things to succeed . . . yet most ads do neither. What's the right strategy?
- Does the Net create a dynamic that fundamentally changes the way everything is marketed?
- How can every business . . . big and small . . . use ideavirus marketing to succeed?

SECTION 1
WHY IDEAS MATTER

Farms, Factories And Idea Merchants

Imagine for a second that you're at your business school reunion, trading lies and bragging about how successful you are and/or are about to become. Frank the jock talks about the dot-com company he just started. Suzie the ex-banker is now focusing her energy on rebuilding Eastern Europe. And then the group looks at you. With a wry look of amusement, you answer:

"Well, the future—the really big money—is in owning a farm. A small one, maybe 100 acres. I intend to invest in a tractor of course, and expect that in just a few years my husband and I can cash out and buy ourselves a nice little brownstone in the city."

Ludicrous, no? While owning a farm may bring tremendous lifestyle benefits, it hasn't been a ticket to wealth for, say, 200 years.

17

What about owning a factory then? Perhaps the road to riches in the new economy would be to buy yourself a hot-stamping press and start turning out steel widgets. Get the UAW to organize your small, dedicated staff of craftsmen and you're on your way to robber-baron status.

Most of us can agree that the big money went out of owning a factory about thirty years ago. When you've got high fixed costs and you're competing against other folks who also know how to produce both quantity and quality, un-seemly profits fly right out the window.

Fact is, the first 100 years of our country's history were about who could build the biggest, most efficient farm. And the second century focused on the race to build factories. Welcome to the third century, folks. The third century is about ideas.

Alas, nobody has a clue how to build a farm for ideas, or even a factory for ideas. We recognize that ideas are driving the economy, ideas are making people rich and most impor-tant, ideas are changing the world. Even though we're clueless about how to best organize the production of ideas, one thing is clear: if you can get people to accept and embrace and adore and cherish your ideas, you win. You win financially, you gain power and you change the world in which we live.

So how do you win? What do you need to do to change the status quo of whatever industry you're in, or, if you're lucky, to change the world?

If you're a farmer, you want nothing more than a high price for your soybeans. If you're a manufacturer of consumer goods, you want a display at the cash register at Wal-Mart. But what if you're an idea merchant?

The holy grail for anyone who traffics in ideas is this: *to unleash an ideavirus.*

An idea that just sits there is worthless. But an idea that moves and grows and infects everyone it touches . . . that's an ideavirus.

In the old days, there was a limit on how many people you could feed with the corn from your farm or the widgets from your factory. But ideas not only replicate easily and well, they get more powerful and more valuable as you deliver them to more people.

How does an ideavirus manifest itself? Where does it live? What does it look like? It's useful to think of ideas of every sort as being similar. I call them manifestos. An idea manifesto is a powerful, logical "essay" that assembles a bunch of existing ideas and creates a new one. Sometimes a manifesto is a written essay. But it can be an image, a song, a cool product or process . . . the medium doesn't matter. The message does. By lumping all sorts of ideas—regardless of format—into the same category (manifestos) it's much easier to think of them as versions of the same thing. As long as

---

DEFINITION: MEDIUM In order to move, an idea has to be encapsulated in a medium. It could be a picture, a phrase, a written article, a movie, even a mathematical formula ($e = mc^2$). The Medium used for transmitting the ideavirus determines how smooth it is as well as the velocity of its growth. A medium is not a manifesto—every idea is a manifesto, trying to make its point, and the medium is the substance that the idea lives in.

you can use your manifesto to change the way people think, talk or act . . . you can create value.

Not only is this book an essay about ideas and idea-viruses, it's also a manifesto striving to become an ideavirus! If this manifesto changes your mind about marketing and ideas, maybe you'll share it with a friend. Or two. Or with your entire company. If that happens, this idea will become an ideavirus, and spread and gain in value.

We live in a world where consumers actively resist marketing. So it's imperative to stop marketing *at* people. The idea is to create an environment where consumers will market to each other.

Is an ideavirus a form of marketing? Sure it is. And today, marketing is all there is. You don't win with better shipping or manufacturing or accounts payable. You win with better marketing, because marketing is about spreading ideas, and ideas are all you've got left to compete with. The future belongs to the people who unleash ideaviruses.

What's an ideavirus? It's a big idea that runs amok across the target audience. It's a fashionable idea that propagates through a section of the population, teaching and changing and influencing everyone it touches. And in our rapidly/instantly changing world, the art and science of building, launching and profiting from ideaviruses is the next frontier.

Have you ever heard of Hotmail? Ever used it? If so, it's not because Hotmail ran a lot of TV ads (they didn't). It's because the manifesto of free email got to you. It turned into an ideavirus. Someone you know and trust infected you with it. What about a Polaroid camera? Was your first exposure (no pun intended!) in a TV ad, or did you discover it when a friend showed you how cool the idea of an instant photograph was?

Sometimes it seems like everyone is watching the same TV show as you, or reading the same book, or talking about the same movie or website. How does that happen? It usually occurs because the idea spreads on its own, through an accidental ideavirus, not because the company behind the product spent a ton of money advertising it or a lot of time orchestrating a virus. And how the idea spreads, and how to make it spread faster—that's the idea behind unleashing an ideavirus.

Word of mouth is not new—it's just different now. There were always ideaviruses—gossip or ideas or politics that spread like wildfire from person to person. Without running an ad or buying a billboard, Galileo managed to upset all of Pisa with his ideas. Today, though, ideaviruses are more important and more powerful than ever. Ideaviruses are easier to launch and more effective. Ideaviruses are critical because they're fast, and speed wins and speed kills—brands and products just don't have the time to develop the old way. Ideaviruses give us increasing returns—word of mouth dies out, but ideaviruses get bigger. And finally, ideaviruses are the currency of the future. While ideaviruses aren't new, they're important because we're obsessed with the new, and an ideavirus is always about the new.

Remember the slogan, "Only her hairdresser knows for sure?" That was classic brand marketing, and it flew in the face of word of mouth. It was an ad for a product that was supposed to be a secret—a secret between you, your hairdresser and Clairol.

A few years later, Herbal Essence took a totally different tack . . . they tried to encourage you to tell your friends. But while word of mouth works great among the people who use a product and their immediate friends—if I love your store or hate your service, I'll tell a few friends—it dies out fast. There's no chance a friend of a friend is going to tell you about my horrible experience on United Airlines or how much I loved flying on Southwest. Word of mouth fades out after a few exchanges.

But now, aided by the Net and abetted by the incredible clutter in our universe, ideaviruses are spreading like wildfire. We're all obsessed with ideas because ideas, not products, are the engine of our new economy.

I wore Converse sneakers growing up—so did you. But the shareholders of Converse never profited from the *idea* of the shoe—they profited from the manufacture of a decent sneaker. If two sneakers were for sale, you bought the cheaper one.

It took Converse generations to build a brand and years to amortize a factory. They were quite happy to extract a modest profit from every pair of sneakers sold because Converse knew their factory would be around tomorrow and the day after that. So sneakers, like everything else, were priced by how much they cost, and sold one pair at a time by earnest shoe salesmen who cared about things like how well the shoes fit.

Converse could take their time. They were in this for the long haul. Those days are long gone. Twenty years later, it's the *idea* of Air Jordan sneakers, not the shoe, that permits Nike to sell them for more than $100. It's the sizzle, not the fit. The *idea* makes Nike outsized profits. And Nike knows that idea won't last long, so they better hurry—they need another ideavirus, fast.

In the old days, we used to sneer at this and call it a fad. Today, everything from presidential politics to music to dentistry is driven by fads—and success belongs to marketers who embrace this fact.

It took 40 years for radio to have ten million users. By then, an industry had grown that could profit from the mass audience. It took 15 years for TV to have 10 million users. It only took 3 years for Netscape to get to 10 million, and it took Hotmail and Napster less than a year. By aggregating mass audiences to themselves (and not having to share them with an entire industry), companies like Netscape and Hotmail are able to realize huge profits, seemingly overnight. And they do it by spreading ideaviruses.

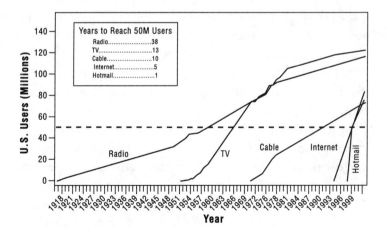

Ideas can now be carried in the ether. Because the medium for carrying ideas is fast and cheap, ideas move faster and cheaper! Whether it's the image of the new VW Beetle (how long did it take for the idea of that car to find a place in your brain?) or the words of a new Stephen King novel (more than 600,000 people read it in the first week it was available online), the time it takes for an idea to circulate is approaching zero.

Why should we care? Why does it matter that ideas can instantly cross international boundaries, change discussions about politics, crime and justice or even get us to buy something? Because the currency of our future is ideas, and the ideavirus mechanism is the way those ideas propagate. And the science and art of creating ideaviruses and using them for profit is new and powerful. You don't have to wait for an ideavirus to happen organically or accidentally. You can plan for it and optimize for it and make it happen.

Sure, some ideaviruses are organic. They happen and spread through no overt action or intent on the part of the person who creates them (the Macarena wasn't an organized plot . . . it just happened). Others, though, are the intentional acts of smart entrepreneurs and politicians who know that launching and nurturing an ideavirus can help them accomplish their goals.

In the old days, the way we sold a product was through interruption marketing. We'd run ads, interrupt people with unanticipated, impersonal, irrelevant ads and hope that they'd buy something. And sometimes, it worked.

The advantage of this branding strategy is that the marketer is in complete and total control. The disadvantage is that it's hard and expensive. Every time a catalog clothier (Land's End, Eddie Bauer, you name it) wants to sign up a new customer, they need to buy a few hundred stamps, send out some carefully designed catalogs and hope that one person sends them money.

What marketers are searching for is a way to circumvent the tyranny of cost-per-thousand interruptions. They need something that ignites, a way to tap into the invisible currents that run between and among consumers, and they need to help those currents move in better, faster, more profitable ways. Instead of always talking *to* consumers, they have to help consumers talk to each other.

A beautifully executed commercial on the Super Bowl is an extraordinarily risky bet. Building a flashy and snazzy website is almost certain to lead to failure. Hiring a celebrity

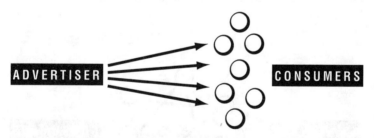

In traditional interruption marketing, the marketer talks directly to as many consumers as possible, with no intermediary other than the media company. The goal of the consumer is to avoid hearing from the advertiser. The goal of the marketer is to spend money buying ads that interrupt people who don't want to be talked to!

spokesperson might work on occasion, but more often than not, it won't break through the clutter. Whenever advertisers build their business around the strategy of talking directly *to* the customer, they become slaves to the math of interruption marketing.

Fortunately, there are already proven techniques you can use to identify, launch and profit from ideas that can be turned into viruses. There's a right and a wrong way to create them, and more important, the care and feeding of your ideavirus can dramatically affect its potency.

One of the key elements in launching an ideavirus is *concentrating* the message. If just 1% or even 15% of a group is excited about your idea, it's not enough. You only win when you totally dominate and amaze the group you've targeted. That's why focusing obsessively on a geographic or demographic or psychographic group is a common trait among successful idea merchants.

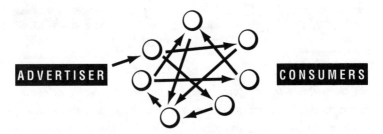

In creating an ideavirus, the advertiser creates an environment in which the idea can replicate and spread. It's the virus that does the work, not the marketer.

Why are new companies launching on the Net so obsessed with traffic and visitors? Why is a company like GeoCities sold for more than $2 billion, when it has close to zero revenue and interesting, but by no means unique, software? Because GeoCities went viral and got bought because they infected the masses.

Infecting large populations with the ideavirus is the first step to building a profitable business model. The key steps for Internet companies looking to build a virus are:

1. Create a noteworthy online experience that's either totally new or makes the user's life much better. Or make an offline experience better/faster/cheaper so that switching is worth the hassle.
2. Have the idea behind your online experience go viral, bringing you a large chunk of the group you're targeting *without* having to spend a fortune advertising the new service.
3. Fill the vacuum in the marketplace with *your* version of the idea, so that competitors now have a very difficult time of unteaching your virus and starting their own.
4. Achieve "lock in" by creating larger and larger costs to switching from your service to someone else's.
5. Get permission from users to maintain an ongoing dialogue so you can turn the original attention into a beneficial experience for users and an ongoing profit stream for you.
6. Continue creating noteworthy online experiences to further spread new viruses, starting with your core audience of raving fans.

Why Are Ideaviruses So Important?

1. We live in a winner-take-almost-all world. (Zipf's law.)
2. We used to focus on making food. We used to make stuff. Now we make ideas.
3. People are more connected than ever. Not only are we more aware that our friends have friends but we can connect with them faster and more frequently.
4. There's a tremendous hunger to understand the new and to remain on the cutting edge.
5. While early adopters (the nerds who always want to know about the cool new thing in their field) have always existed, now we've got more nerds than ever. *If you're reading this, you're a nerd!*
6. The profit from creating and owning an ideavirus is huge.

Five Things Ideaviruses Have In Common

1. The most successful ideaviruses sometimes appear to be accidents, but it is possible to dramatically increase the chances your ideavirus will catch on and spread.
2. An ideavirus adores a vacuum. (This is a big idea. Read on to see what I mean).
3. Once an ideavirus spreads, it follows a lifecycle. Ignore the lifecycle and the ideavirus dies out. Feed it properly and you can extend its useful life and profit from it for a long time.
4. Ideaviruses are more than just essays and books. Everything from new technology to new ways of creating new

products are winning because of intelligent seeding by their creators.

5. Viral marketing is a special case of an ideavirus. Viral marketing is an ideavirus in which the carrier of the virus *is* the product.

Seven Ways An Ideavirus Can Help You

1. When everyone in town tells ten friends about your amazing ice cream shop and a line forms out the door (supercharged word of mouth due to the virus having dominated the town so completely).
2. When your company's new mass storage format catches on and it becomes the next Zip drive.
3. When an influential sports writer names your daughter as a high school All-American basketball player and coaches line up outside the door with scholarships.
4. When Steve Jobs commissions the iMac, which spreads the word about the Mac faster than any advertising ever could, raising market share and saving your favorite computer company from bankruptcy.
5. When you write a report for your boss about how your company should deal with an opportunity in Cuba and it gets passed on, from person to person, throughout the company, making you a hero and a genius.
6. When the demo recording you made becomes a bestseller on MP3.com and you get a call from Sony, who wants to give you a recording contract.
7. When you are able to devise a brand-new Internet business plan for a product that's useful and also embodies

viral marketing—growing from nothing to a million users in a month and making you rich along the way.

The Sad Decline of Interruption Marketing

When I first starting writing about Permission Marketing about four years ago, much of what I said was considered heresy. "What do you mean TV ads are going to decline in effectiveness?" "How dare you say anything negative about banner ads—of course they work!" or "Direct mail has never been healthier!"

History, fortunately for me, has borne out my cries of doom and gloom about interruption marketing. The TV networks are diversifying away from their traditional network TV business as fast as they can. Banner clickthrough rates are down 85% or more. Ads are sprouting up on the floors of the supermarket, in the elevator of the Hilton hotel in Chicago and even in urinals. And everywhere you look, unanticipated, impersonal and irrelevant ads are getting more expensive and less effective.

There's a crisis in interruption marketing and it's going to get much worse. It took more than thirty pages to build the case against this wasteful, costly ($220 billion a year) outmoded expense in *Permission Marketing,* so I'll only spend a page on it here. If you want to read the entire jeremiad, send a note to free@permission.com and I'll send it to you for free.

Unless you find a more cost-effective way to get your message out, your business is doomed. You can no longer survive by interrupting strangers with a message they don't want to hear, about a product they've never heard of, using methods that annoy them. Consumers have too little time and too much power to stand for this any longer.

We Live In A Winner-Take-Almost-All World

Quick! Name an oil painting hanging in a museum somewhere in the world.

Did you say, "the Mona Lisa"?

As I walk through the Louvre, arguably one of the top ten most packed-with-high-quality-paintings museums on the planet, I pass one empty room after another, then come to an alcove packed with people. Why? Why are these people clawing all over each other in order to see a painting poorly displayed behind many inches of bullet-proof glass?

The reason the Mona Lisa is the most famous painting in the world is that *something* had to be the most famous painting in the world and it might as well be the Mona Lisa.

Busy people don't have time to look at every painting. They only have room in their overcrowded, media-hyped

brains for a few paintings. And when you come right down to it, most people would like to see only the "celebrity" paintings. And just as there can only be one "My most favorite famous actress" (Julia Roberts) and one "this site equals the Internet" (Yahoo!), there's only room for one "most famous painting in the world" and the safe choice is the Mona Lisa.

There's a name for this effect. It's called Zipf's law, after George Kingsley Zipf (1902–1950), a philologist and professor at Harvard University. He discovered that the most popular word in the English language ("the") is used ten times more than the tenth most popular word, 100 times more than the 100th most popular word and 1,000 times more than the 1,000th most popular word.

It's also been discovered that this same effect applies to market share for software, soft drinks, automobiles, candy bars, and the frequency of hits on pages found on a website. The chart following shows actual visits to the different pages at a typical website (Sun Microsystems):

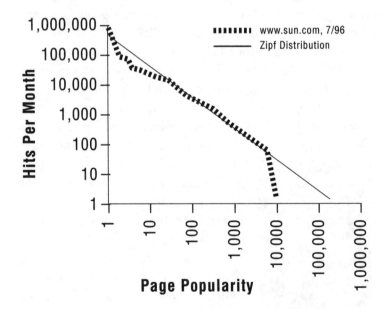

In almost every field of endeavor, it's clear that being #1 is a *lot* better than being #3 or #10. There isn't an even distribution of rewards, especially in our networked world.

On the Net, the stakes are even larger. The market capitalization of Priceline, eBay and Amazon approaches 95% of the total market capitalization of every other consumer e-commerce stock *combined*. Clearly, there's a lot to be gained by winning.

An ideavirus lets you make something like this happen to your idea, to your business, to your product. While the benefits of being #1 for a public Internet stock or an oil painting are clear, it's just as important to small businesses and individuals.

Ideaviruses are faced with a brickwall filter. In electronics, a brickwall filter wipes out certain frequencies and lets the rest through. There's no room for second place or extra effort—either you're in or you're out. Ideaviruses are win/lose propositions. Either the velocity and smoothness are high enough that it becomes a bonafide epidemic, or they're not and it dies out. Either your ideavirus works or it doesn't. Smart propagators know when to quit if their ideavirus isn't getting through the filter.

DEFINITION: VELOCITY The velocity is a measure of how fast the idea spreads from one party to another. If an idea is going to hit ten people before it gets to me, the multiplier effect is large indeed—fast steps lead to more people being infected before it dies out.

DEFINITION: SMOOTHNESS How easy is it for an end user to spread this particular ideavirus? Can I click one button or mention some magic phrase, or do I have to go through hoops and risk embarrassment to tell someone about it?

For example, it's pretty easy to talk about your hairdresser. Someone tells you you've got a great haircut, and you say, "Yeah, I went to Bob at Bumble & Bumble." On the other hand, spreading the word about your reflexology therapist is pretty tricky. You're not sure when to bring it up, and you really don't have words to describe it.

The smoothest viruses, like Hotmail, spread themselves. Just the act of using the product spreads the virus. There's an obvious relationship between smoothness and catchiness. A product that's easy to recommend is often a product that's easy to get hooked on.

Eric Raymond was a little known programmer when he wrote an essay called "The Cathedral and the Bazaar." It was a manifesto—an essay designed to become an ideavirus—arguing why the open source approach to coding (creating stuff like Linux) made sense. But instead of having a magazine or a book publisher bring it to market, he posted the essay online, in text, postscript and audio form. And he gave it away for free.

Within months, tens of thousands of people had read it. Months after that, Raymond published this essay with some of his other free essays in a book. That book became an "instant" bestseller. Of course, it wasn't instant at all. He had laid the foundation long before, by building an ideavirus.

So, what has creating an ideavirus done for Raymond's value? Let's take a crass look at his financial situation: The virus led to increased demand for his services as a programmer (he can pick his jobs if he likes), as a consultant, and even as a public speaker. The last I saw, he had just written an essay about what it was like to make a fortune during an IPO!

The Traffic Imperative: Why Sites Fail

According to Forrester Research, only 20% of 50 leading online retailers expect to turn a profit this year. Just 18% more expect to be profitable next year. It's becoming increasingly obvious that many of these sites will *never* turn a profit, and that they're hoping to last long enough to be acquired or sell their stock.

A recent McKinsey and Co. study found that the vast majority of online retailers are not only unprofitable, they're actually losing money on every sale. Without even computing the cost of advertising and clicks, these sites have discounted their prices so significantly that the contribution margin from each sale is negative. The average online drugstore, for example, loses $16.42 on each and every sale, before computing the cost of traffic.

Why? Many of these sites are confusing low prices with an effective customer acquisition tool. There's probably no way that's less effective and more costly than cutting your prices to the point where you lose money on each sale (for Amazon naysayers—they actually make a profit of about $5 on the average book order).

DEFINITION: HIVE People are not one amorphous mass. We're self-organized into groups, or hives that have several things in common: a way to communicate among ourselves; spoken or unspoken rules and standards; and a common history. Some examples: Fraternity brothers, orthodox Jews, readers of *Fast Company*, Deadheads.

Add to this mess the obscene cost of customer acquisition—estimated by the Boston Consulting Group to be more than $80 a visitor (that's for *visitors*, not even customers) for most online merchants. Now you can see the huge hurdle these sites are going to have to cross in order to be profitable.

This problem isn't unique to the online world, of course. When I was enrolled at Tufts University in 1980, there were two homemade ice cream stores within two miles of campus. One was Joey's, which made a terrific product (they used Hydrox cookies instead of Oreos), and there was never, ever a line.

In the other direction was the now famous Steve's Ice Cream. His prices were a bit higher than Joey's, but his profits were clearly much higher. Why? Because there was always a line at Steve's. A long line. Sometimes you'd wait an hour to get an ice cream cone.

What happened? Why did one ice cream shop go viral and the other languish at the edge of profitability? It certainly wasn't about advertising, because neither shop did any. The reason Steve Herrell's shop did so well is that it was famous for having a line! People brought folks from out of town to have the experience. Locals came back because they'd convinced themselves that if the hive liked it enough to wait an hour for an ice cream cone, well, it must be worth it. Suddenly, it wasn't about the ice cream. It was about the experience.

Most online merchants, being risk averse copycats afraid to innovate, are guaranteeing that there will be no ideavirus created around their businesses. By paying millions to AOL and Yahoo! for "traffic," they're investing in exactly the wrong sort of buzz. The alternative—focusing on people who can promote your site, affiliate programs, unique promotions and building wow, zing and magic into the site—is just too much work for most sites.

We Used To Make Food. We Used To Make Stuff. Now We Make Ideas.

Here are some astonishing facts you should think about long and hard on your way to work tomorrow: Twenty years ago, the top 100 companies in the Fortune 500 either dug something out of the ground or turned a natural resource (iron ore or oil) into something you could hold. Today, fewer than half of the companies on the list do that. The rest make unseemly profits by trafficking in ideas. In 1998, there were 30,000 new musical CDs published, including one from the Pope (his, which I like a lot, features a little rap, a little techno and a lot of worldbeats).

Ninety-nine percent of Yahoo's market capitalization is due to brand, sizzle, user loyalty and other "soft" ideas. Only 1% of the company's value is due to actual unique stuff that you can't get anywhere else.

Nathan Mhyrvold, former chief scientist at Microsoft, says a great programmer is worth 10,000 times more than an average one. Why? Because of the quality of her ideas.

The important takeaway is this: Ideas aren't a sideshow that make our factory a little more valuable. Our factory is a sideshow that makes our ideas a little more valuable!

People Are More Connected Than They Ever Were Before. We Have Dramatically More Friends Of Friends And We Can Connect With Them Faster And More Frequently Than Ever.

Think back. Really far. Ten years ago.

How many people did you have regular telephone contact with ten years ago? Probably ten or twenty or thirty in your personal life, and maybe 100 at work?

Now, take a look at your email inbox or your instant messenger buddy list. How many people do you hear from every week?

We're far more connected than we ever were. And now, we've got second or third or fourth order connections. There's an email in my box from someone who is married to someone I went to summer camp with twenty years ago who got my email address from a third friend.

Another message is from a former employee, telling me about a doctor who's about to lose his license for trying radical medical treatments, and how her mother-in-law will suffer if this guy can't practice any longer.

It's hard for me to imagine either person contacting me if they had to walk across the village and bang on the door of my hut or pick up the phone and call me. But the moment you connect to the Internet, you connect, at some level, to all of us. And the connections make ideas travel. Fast.

What's the difference between word of mouth and an ideavirus? Two differences. First, word of mouth tends to spread slower, be more analog. If you like a book, you might tell a friend or two. And then your friends are unlikely to tell someone else until they read it for themselves.

Second, word of mouth dies off. Because the numbers are smaller, it doesn't take many people who don't participate in the word of mouth for each generation to be smaller than the one before it.

With an ideavirus, both principles no longer apply. Ideaviruses spread fast and they spread far. With word of mouse (word of mouth augmented by the power of online communication), you can tell 100 friends, or a thousand friends.

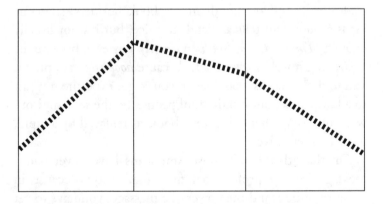

Here's a schematic of typical word of mouth. Notice how few cycles there are, and how it drops off over time.

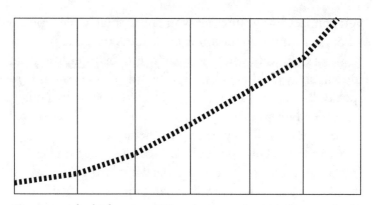

Here's an ideal ideavirus. Note how much more frequently the cycles occur, and how each cycle sees the virus grow.

Because the numbers are larger and faster, the virus grows instead of slows.

Even before the Net, there were special cases of viruses. In traditional word of mouth in the book business, someone reads a book and tells a friend. It's nice, but it's not usually enough. *The Bridges of Madison County,* however, became the bestselling novel of the decade, because *booksellers* adopted it and told people. As a bookseller, you've got exposure not just to a few people, but hundreds of people. So the serendipitous word of mouth that helps some books is replaced by a rapid, virulent alternative.

On the other hand, most Americans have never had a massage from a professional masseuse. Why? Because in order to understand the power of a massage, you have to get one. We don't currently have the word or picture tools to adequately describe the positive benefits of a massage, and just as important, there isn't a powerful spokesperson for massage who has spent the time and energy to develop the ideavirus. There's no real medium to transmit the message. The message travels slowly. So there is no virus around the idea of a massage.

There's A Tremendous Hunger To Understand The New And To Remain On The Cutting Edge.

Jed Clampett discovered that finding oil on his property was a sure road to riches. Today, the road seems to be paved with awareness. If you know what's news, if you know what's the latest, hottest, most impactful new idea, it's much easier to succeed. You can profit in the stock market, do better in politics, find breakthroughs in science, or programming or marketing.

Why does this matter? Because in a society where the new isn't valued, your social standing doesn't increase when you become a nerd. And because ideaviruses are really nothing but amplified gossip about new stuff, they can't take root in a culture that doesn't care about the new.

Take a look at the Top 40 charts in Billboard magazine. Thirty or forty years ago, a record could easily stay on the list for six months or more. Today, new records come and go much faster. Why? Because we are happily saturated in the current hit, and then move on.

Last year, 1,778 business books were published in the U.S. alone. Every one of them got read by someone, some by an awful lot of people. Why? Because as our world changes faster and faster and faster, *knowing* is just as important as having.

And that makes the population ready and eager for the next ideavirus.

As the speed of new ideas entering the community has increased, so has our respect for people who know. And because it's valuable, we're open to both hearing about the new and telling others about it.

While Early Adopters (The Nerds Who Always Want To Know About The Cool New Thing In Their Field) Have Always Existed, Now We've Got More Nerds Than Ever Before. *If You're Reading This, You're A Nerd!*

The Internet turned us all into nerds. AltaVista isn't cool any more—Google.com is. Don't use the Palm, that's passé. Try this Handspring instead. Suddenly we're ready, willing and able to be at the bleeding edge, all the time.

The profit from creating and owning an ideavirus is huge, bigger than it ever was before. It used to be that only a few stereotypical nerds cared about the latest pocket calculator. Today, you'll see people talking about their handheld computer on the subway. It used to be that only a few people knew about the latest salsa hit out of Mexico or the coolest new chef in Los Angeles. Today, the roles are totally reversed. Your parents are nerds!

It's not just that our society is rewarding people who are sensitive enough or smart enough or cool enough to know about the next new thing. It's that many of us have crossed over a line and gone from being the vast majority who waited for something to become mainstream—we've become the early adopters, the folks on the bleeding edge who actually seek out innovation. The combined circulation of *Wired, Fast Company* and *PC Magazine* is rapidly approaching the total circulation of *Sports Illustrated.*

Because the population has shifted, the sweet spot has shifted. Companies no longer make most of their money harvesting money from the laggards who finally get around to buying something at K-Mart. They make their money the first day, the first week, the first month an idea is out there.

If something is new and different and exciting and getting buzzed about, we want to know about it, be part of it. The fashion is now to be in fashion, and ideas are the way we keep up.

Ideas Are More Than Just Essays And Books. Everything From New Technology To New Ways Of Creating, To New Products Are Winning Because Of Intelligent Ideavirus Management By Their Creators.

A manifesto is a carefully organized series of ideas, designed to get someone to come around to your point of view. But while one way to make a complicated argument is with a book, you can just as easily (and sometimes more effectively) send it through a song (Bob Dylan did this for Hurricane Carter) or with something as elegant as an OXO vegetable peeler.

When you first see the OXO, you instantly understand the idea behind it. You just know it will work better and cut you less often. If you've ever peeled a vegetable, *you want an OXO.* The design of the OXO is quite simply a manifesto that says, "There's a smart, comfortable way to do this annoying task."

Is the OXO going to get viral? Not across the general population, of course, but if you hang out with a group of people who have arthritis or love kitchen stuff, it already has. Just take a look at the glowing reviews of this peeler on Amazon's kitchen site.

The End Of The Zero Sum Game

Traditional advertising is a game with winners and losers. If your product gets attention from the targeted consumer, you win "mindshare" and your customer loses time. When a consumer is foolish enough to listen to an irrelevant ad, she loses time and doesn't even gain useful information. It's an old economy model in which every transaction has someone *taking* something.

Permission marketing and the ideavirus are both very different from this model. These models create a game in which everyone can win! If there's a great idea, and it moves through the hive for free, everyone who touches it wins in several ways.

First, you as the consumer win for recommending it to a friend. This increases your status as a powerful sneezer (or your compensation as a promiscuous sneezer.) Because you

DEFINITION: SNEEZER Some people are more likely to tell their friends about a great new idea. These people are at the heart of the ideavirus. Identifying and courting sneezers is a key success factor for idea merchants.

respect your peers, you're not suggesting or pitching something that doesn't make your friends' lives better. Violate this respect and your power as a sneezer goes way down.

Second, the recipient benefits as well. He benefits from the way the idea changes his life, and he benefits because he now has the ability to sneeze the idea to someone else, thus increasing his power.

Third, the creator of the idea succeeds because her idea propagates and because she can sell souvenirs (speeches, consulting, value-added services) to people who are now open and receptive to her idea.

My friend, Chris Meyer, co-author of *Blur,* had this to say: "The one thing that distinguishes effective sneezing campaigns from ineffective ones is *respect* for the time, attention, and reputation of the next guy to catch the virus. It's important to note that the decision to sneeze is, in general, a distributed one, made by each of us as to whether to clog our friend's email or whatever with the virus in question, because our (local, at least) reputation is at stake."

This insight goes to the core of why ideaviruses are succeeding and why traditional marketers don't immediately grasp this approach (or permission marketing for that matter.) The distributed nature of the decision is the antithesis of the command-and-control General Patton approach that marketers have taken previously.

The reason that *The Red Herring, The Industry Standard* and other magazines are jammed with ads is not because the ads always work. They don't. The reason the ads are purchased is that in exchange for money the marketer gets the illusion that they're in charge of the conversation, at least for a few seconds.

Bill Bernbach, the dean of American Advertising, was co-founder of DDB Advertising. He died twenty years ago, but before he left us, he pointed the way to this "new" way of marketing:

> "You cannot sell a man who isn't listening; word of mouth is the best medium of all; and dullness won't sell your product, but neither will irrelevant brilliance."

The answer, of course, is to give people a reason to listen and then create an infrastructure that will amplify their ability to spread word of mouth. And core to both of those tasks is the new respect that marketers need to show newly powerful consumers.

SECTION 2

HOW TO UNLEASH
AN IDEAVIRUS

**While It May Appear Accidental, It's Possible To Dramatically
Increase The Chances Your Ideavirus Will Catch On And Spread.**

This is the really cool part. Once you understand the fundamental elements behind the propagation of an ideavirus, you can unleash your own.

Just because ideaviruses have usually spread through unknown means or accidental events doesn't mean that there isn't a science to building and managing them.

You can invest in designing your product to make it virusworthy. Then if you understand the eight elements of the ideavirus formula, you increase your chances of spreading your ideavirus with every step along the way.

This can change the way you approach all of your marketing. If launching an ideavirus is the most powerful thing you can do for a product and service, and there are steps you can take to increase the likelihood that this will occur, you've got to try!

The Heart Of The Ideavirus: Sneezers

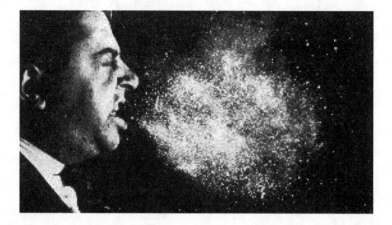

Some people are far more likely to spread an ideavirus than others. Malcolm Gladwell (author of the brilliant book and ideavirus, *The Tipping Point*) calls this the Law of the Few and breaks the key virus spreaders into three groups: Connectors, Mavens and Salespeople. What's critical in the analysis is understanding that some folks are dead ends, while others will enable and amplify your ideavirus.

In his best example, Gladwell talks about the success of Paul Revere in warning us that the British were coming. It turns out that a second man, William Dawes, went on a similar ride the same night—but his was a total failure.

Why did Dawes fail where Revere succeeded? It's because people knew Paul Revere. They trusted him. He had credibility. And so when he said something, people were willing to listen and believe. Revere was a sneezer. Dawes, a loner, tried hard but couldn't get the idea to become a virus.

Sneezers are at the core of any ideavirus. Sneezers are the ones who when they tell ten or twenty or 100 people—people *believe* them.

Sneezers Are So Important, We Need To Subdivide Them.

There are two basic kinds of sneezers:

Promiscuous Sneezers
This is your uncle the insurance salesman. The promiscuous sneezers are members of a hive who can be counted on to try to "sell" their favorite ideavirus to almost anyone, almost any time.

* Promiscuous sneezers can be motivated by money or other inducements.
* Promiscuous sneezers are rarely held in high esteem as opinion leaders, but if they're promiscuous enough, they can be extremely effective.

Many of the Net businesses that are now being organized around ideaviruses are targeting this group (people who are willing to sell to their friends for personal gain). Companies like Mercata.com, Alladvantage.com and even Amazon.com are offering inducements to customers that compensate them for spreading ideas to their friends and acquaintances

in an attempt to acquire new customers. As the value of creating ideaviruses increases, we'll see more of this, and we'll also see more and more people becoming promiscuous sneezers—basically, we're paying folks enough to corrupt them into spreading ideas in exchange for cash.

Powerful Sneezers
The hat business is near the end of an eighty-year downward spiral to total irrelevance. Each year has brought worse news, with one manufacturer after another going out of business, and most towns left with one (if they're lucky) haberdasher.

In the midst of all this dismal news, about twenty years ago there was one bright spot: Harrison Ford. With a bullwhip. Wearing a hat.

Ford's Indiana Jones sold more hats for Stetson than any single person since the invention of the Marlboro Man. Why? Because Ford has the influence to set style, because his appearance in a movie wearing that hat coaxed millions of men who wanted to be like him into buying a hat.

The paradox of the powerful sneezer is that he can't be bought. Every time a powerful sneezer accepts a bribe in exchange for spreading a virus, his power decreases. When Bruce

Springsteen does ads in Japan, or Whoopi Goldberg shills for Flooz, they have less leverage as powerful sneezers. The public knows that they can be motivated by more than just taste.

In fact, every time a powerful sneezer tries something new and introduces a new idea, she takes a risk. If her followers reject the virus (for whatever reason), her ability to introduce future viruses decreases. For this reason, it's difficult to manipulate powerful sneezers, and equally difficult to predict what might motivate them to adopt an ideavirus.

Here's an analogy that demonstrates the difference between promiscuous sneezers and powerful sneezers, and more important, explains how they might converge:

Anyone can buy an ad in the Pennysaver, or even write and insert a "special advertising section" in some fancy magazine. The advantage of this kind of presentation, obviously, is that it gives the marketer complete control over how the message appears and what it says. Advertising is basically paid sneezing. And because the public realizes that that's all it is, it doesn't have an awful lot of credibility. It still works, but it's not as effective as real sneezing from a powerful sneezer.

On the other hand, it's up to the editor in chief of the *New York Times* to decide what articles appear in the paper. No matter how much money a marketer spends (even though spending a lot might get you noticed by the editorial staff), there's no guarantee that an article will appear— and no guarantee that if it does appear, it will say what you want it to say.

Enter the web. There are plenty of websites where the line between editorial content and advertising is blurred, where sponsoring a website also gives you the right to say what you want to say.

So let's imagine for a second that the *New York Times* embraced this shocking idea. Imagine they said, "Okay marketers, write your own articles! And pay us to run them!" Now there'd be some ground rules. First, the marketer would specify how much they'd be willing to pay to have a story featured. For example, a restaurant could decide it might be worth $10,000 for a feature on their new chef to appear in print.

Second, the *Times* would get final say over what was printed.

Obviously, a wholesale switch from powerful sneezer to promiscuous sneezer would decimate the circulation base of the *Times*. If the *Times* accepted any article, regardless of credibility and interest, just because the marketer was the highest bidder, it would totally destroy the paper within a week.

But what if the *Times* realized that picking only the very best articles that were submitted (maybe just a few a day) could ensure that people would still be delighted to read the paper? What if the *Times* knew that for every 199 badly written restaurant fluff pieces, a great one would show up? And what if the editor in chief had enough guts to pick just the great articles and resist pressure to completely sell out?

Journalistic handwringing aside, this is already happening (not at the fabled *Times,* of course), and it's going to happen more. It's happening on websites. It's happening on television (witness the CBS coverage of iWon.com awarding prizes—CBS owns a chunk of iWon.) And far more interesting than this tortured analogy, it's already happening with people's personal sneezing ethics.

A hundred years ago, there weren't many opportunities for playwrights, actors and captains of industry to sell out. Today, Whoopi Goldberg pitches Flooz, William Shatner pitches Priceline and Gerald Ford is on the board of directors of several companies. In each case, the celebrity is shifting from role of influential, powerful, can't-be-bought-I'm-a-style-statesman to promiscuous sneezer, available for sale. William Shatner had lost his ability to set style through his actions—he was past his prime as a powerful sneezer. So the segue to paid sneezer made sense for his career. It would probably be a dumb move for Tom Cruise or Mel Gibson, though.

After I left Yahoo!, I had many opportunities to serve on boards and do endorsements. I chose not to. Why? Because I didn't want to squander the powerful sneezing points I'd earned by writing my last book. The one ad I did, I did for free. And I'm still hearing about it.

Think about your own situation. Have you ever signed up a friend for MCI's Friends and Family program? Or tried to get someone to use your Amazon affiliate links to buy books, or join with you to buy something at Mercata.com? In every case, you're getting paid to alter your behavior. That makes you more promiscuous and less powerful.

As the Net makes it easier to measure ideaviruses and motivate sneezers, we're going to see far more people become promiscuous sneezers, but, at the same time, the role of the powerful sneezer will become ever more important. As available attention becomes ever more precious, we're going to be far more likely to listen to someone who's spreading a virus for non-personal gain.

Epinions.com is a fascinating model of the intersection between the powerful and the promiscuous sneezers. Here's a site where hundreds of thousands of people come to hear the opinions of thousands of sneezers. Everything is reviewed, from books to dishwashers. And the reviewers are clearly identified and constantly ranked. Promiscuous sneezers (who get paid to do the reviews) suddenly become powerful! How? If a lot of people read and like your reviews, your reviews carry more weight, regardless of your compensation scheme.

"Xyz" has posted more than 1,000 reviews and been read more than 100,000 times. She's compensated every time someone reads one of her reviews, so she certainly qualifies as promiscuous. She works hard to get others to read her reviews. But at the same time, she's developing a reputation as a powerful sneezer.

Referrals.com is a business based around the idea of paying people to help with job searches. Instead of just giving some headhunter the names of five friends who might be perfect for a job (and having the headhunter collect a $30,000 fee if you're right), Referrals.com turns the idea upside down. With their system, *you* send the job offer along to your friends, and if they take the job, you get a check for $4,000.

If Referrals.com only attracts promiscuous sneezers, the business will fail. Why? Because the very best people try hard not to listen to interruptions from promiscuous sneezers. The very best people know that if someone can be bought, they're not much more than a walking billboard, and just as they ignore the billboards on the highway, they're going to ignore the most promiscuous sneezers in their midst. (Aside: If you've ever been called by a headhunter, you know just how promiscuous people are willing to be in exchange for cash!)

Referrals.com is working very hard to turn powerful sneezers within very select, high-end hives into people who, on occasion, are willing to sell out for a $4,000 payoff. These are folks who might not hassle you just so they can make $5 or $10 in bonuses. But the idea of becoming a headhunter and making $4,000 in exchange for sending a few emails is too irresistible to pass up. This idea that even the powerful can become promiscuous for the right inducement and in the right setting is a key building block to unleashing the ideavirus in an organized way.

What a paradox. Powerful sneezers become less powerful when you buy them off. But sometimes, promiscuous sneezers become powerful again when they get particularly successful at it. It's a cycle, with people switching off from one to another, always trying to figure out how to be both promiscuous (read profitable) and powerful.

The Art Of The Promiscuous

How do you attract and keep promiscuous sneezers? There are six key principles:

1. Make big promises.
2. Show them how to make it up in volume.
3. Describe an attainable path.
4. When one succeeds, tell the rest of them.

5. Give the successful ones a way to show the non-sneezers it worked.

6. Have a Mary Kay convention.

Make big promises

One of the things that drives someone to become a promiscuous sneezer is the opportunity for a change in lifestyle. Certain rewards, though small, are not as enticing as slightly less certain rewards that are much larger. Human nature (especially among the optimists) will give you the benefit of the doubt on the risks, but it won't cut you any slack on the rewards.

So, I'm much more likely to help you out for a chance to get free dry cleaning for six months than I am to get a certain reward of $4 off my next dry cleaning bill.

Show them how to make it up in volume

Of course, the promise has to be believable. One of the best ways to do that is to make it clear to the promiscuous sneezer that the system can be gamed. Let them know that if they work the system, the odds of winning go way up.

If I look at the offer you make and say, "Wait. If I go to *ten* friends, not just one, then I'm a lock to win this great prize . . ." you've done it right. I may think I'm scamming you by going to so many people to adjust the odds in my favor, but actually, I'm doing just what you wanted me to do—and then some.

Many of the online affiliate programs work this way. These programs offer a commission for referrals that result in a sale. First designed as a cheap way to get new customers referred from relevant web sites, they've evolved into something far bigger. If you're at an online pet store, for example, and you see a link to a book about training dogs, you can click on the link and buy it from Amazon.com. Amazon then sends the affiliate (the online pet store) a commission. Small businesspeople have looked at these programs and said "Wait! If I build a site that does nothing but sell books and Barnes and Noble does all the work, I'll scam the system and make a ton of money." Of course, the online bookstore doesn't care a wit about where the customers come from. They're just happy to have them. In essence, hundreds of thousands of entrepreneurs are now building businesses dedicated to finding customers for other merchants.

Describe an attainable path

Alas, trust is in short supply, even among optimistic promiscuous sneezers. Thus you've got to make it clear to potential sneezers that there is in fact a way for them to profit from this adventure.

This is especially true for offers where you don't have a lot of time to make your case. By showing the sneezer how smooth the system is, by making it trivially easy to forward that email or whisper to that friend, you're far more likely to get their initial enthusiasm. The first few sneezes are the most difficult to get an individual to perform.

When one succeeds, tell the rest of them

This is so important and so overlooked. I'm presuming that you've gained permission to talk with your sneezers on an ongoing basis. So now talk to them! I'm a member of several online affiliate programs, but not one of them does this. Why not send announcements detailing how the most effective affiliates are doing? Why not invite me to visit their sites and see them in action? By making it really clear that some sneezers are happily profiting, you dramatically increase the chances you'll get better performance from the rest of your sneezers.

Give the successful ones a way to show the non-sneezers it worked

Mary Kay cosmetics gives its best salespeople a pink Cadillac. This is no accident.

There are plenty of ways to pay off a promiscuous sneezer. Why do it with a pink Cadillac? Because it is a persistent amplifier of this sneezer's success. Because it attracts new sneezers to the fold. Because it's proof to the rest of your organization and to the world that you can get rich by selling cosmetics to your friends.

Have a Mary Kay convention

Just because it's a new century doesn't mean we should abandon the idea of getting together in real life. Zig Ziglar tells the story of how Mary Kay went to a sales convention when she was a struggling salesperson. She didn't even have enough money to eat the meals there . . . she brought her own crackers and cheese. But at the final banquet, when the salespeople queued up to shake the company president's hand, Mary Kay looked at him and said, "Next year, I'll be back as the #1 salesperson." The president, who could have easily brushed off the claim, stopped what he was doing, paused for a full thirty seconds, looked her in the eye and said, "Yes, yes, I believe you will."

And the rest is sales history. But without the convention, I seriously doubt this would have occurred. *How can* you *get together with* your *best promiscuous sneezers?*

In addition to these six principles, there are two things you can do to totally and completely wreck your network of promiscuous sneezers:

- Change the rules in the middle
- View the relationship as an expense

Don't change the rules in the middle

Alladvantage.com is one of the fastest growing websites on the planet. The idea was to create a multi-level marketing organization where each member would get paid for the ads they saw and, more importantly, for the ads seen by the people they recruited. This led to a classic MLM (multi-level marketing) network marketing business, where people made more money bringing in new salespeople than they did actually using the product.

After growing to more than five million registered users, the company took a look at the numbers and realized that the path to profitability was going to be hampered by the high rates they were paying. So, well within the fine print they had published when they first started, they changed the rates.

All hell broke loose. The very best sneezers started sneezing *against* the company. The growth rate hiccupped. Bad news. They'll survive, and they might even continue their record growth. But far better to have run the numbers in advance and had a payment schedule they could live with forever.

Don't view the relationship as an expense

It's so easy to move your relationship with promiscuous sneezers from investment to expense. After all, at the beginning it's great because these people are dramatically cutting your acquisition costs and helping you grow. But once you do grow, it's easy to assume your growth might be able to continue without the "high cost" of paying your sneezers.

In practice, there are two terrible side effects. The first is that you'll inevitably try to trim the benefits you offer your sneezers as well as the effort you put into keeping them happy. Better to just cancel the program outright than to start disappointing these critical allies (remember, an unhappy promiscuous sneezer can quickly become an angry powerful sneezer).

Second, you'll find yourself trying to grow using techniques that you haven't evolved, tested, measured or practiced. And more often than not, that means failure.

A better strategy is to put a cap on your new sneezer acquisition efforts at the same time you love and reward your existing sneezers. During this interregnum period, get really good at tapping other ways to grow. Only after you're confident that you've got the transition working should you start to phase out the sneezers who got you there in the first place.

It's More Than Just Word Of Mouth

Marketers have been pursuing word of mouth for years. There are five important principles that someone unleashing an ideavirus should understand—principles that marketers pursuing old-fashioned word of mouth didn't use:

1. An idea merchant understands that creating the virus is the single most important part of her job. So she'll spend all her time and money on creating a product and environment that feeds the virus.

2. An idea merchant understands that by manipulating the key elements of idea propagation—the velocity, the vector, the smoothness, the persistence and the identification of sneezers—she can dramatically alter a virus's success.

DEFINITION: VECTOR As an ideavirus moves through a population, it usually follows a vector. It could be a movement toward a certain geographic or demographic audience, for example. Sometimes an ideavirus starts in a sub-group and then breaks through that niche into the public consciousness. Other times, it works its way through a group and then just stops. Napster vectored straight to college kids. Why? Because they combined the three things necessary for the virus to catch on: fast connection, spare time and an obsession with new music.

> DEFINITION: PERSISTENCE Some ideas stick around a long time with each person, influencing them (and those they sneeze on) for months or years to come. Others have a much shorter half-life before they fade out.

3. The idea merchant remembers that digital word of mouth is a permanent written record online, a legacy that will follow the product, for good or for ill, forever.

4. An idea merchant realizes that the primary goal of a product or service is not just to satisfy the needs of one user. It has to deliver so much wow, be so cool, so neat and so productive that the user tells five friends. *Products market themselves by creating and reinforcing ideaviruses.*

5. An idea merchant knows that the ideavirus follows a lifecycle and decides at which moment to shift from *paying* to spread it, to *charging* the user and profiting from it.

An Ideavirus Adores A Vacuum

It's very hard to keep two conflicting ideaviruses in your head at the same time (Communism: evil or benign? Martha Stewart: pro or con? Can't have both). So if an idea already inhabits space in your consumer's brain, your idea can't peacefully coexist. It usually has to dislodge a different idea, the incumbent, and that's always tough.

Given that, the best friend of an ideavirus is a vacuum. When "60 Minutes" ran the story about runaway acceleration in Audi cars, it was an ideal ideavirus. Why? Because most people had never driven an Audi. Most people had never interacted with the Audi company. Most people didn't have a best friend who loved his Audi. As a result, the virus rushed in, filled the vacuum and refused to be dislodged.

Audi, of course, did exactly the wrong thing in fighting the virus. They issued a tight-lipped response and relied on engineering data to *prove* that they were right. Very correct, very German and totally ineffective. It cost the company billions of dollars in lost sales.

Audi didn't have to go out and spread the idea that Audis were good cars. That would have been pretty straightforward if they were starting from scratch. Instead, Audi had to *undo* the idea that had been spread by "60 Minutes." And responding "did not" to TV's "did too" was a recipe for failure.

Instead, they could have countered the virus by filling in the rest of the vacuum. I would have advised them to put an Audi 5000 in every major shopping mall in America. Let people sit in it. Invite them to take the "Audi Sudden Acceleration Test" and see for themselves what the car was like. By creating a more vivid and forceful alternative to a television hatchet job, Audi could have unleashed its own countervirus.

At the beginning, the Internet was a vacuum. A Yahoo! or an eBay or an Amazon could walk in and propagate its ideavirus fast and cheap. Today, though, launching a new search engine or a new email service is hard indeed. Why? Because the vacuum's gone.

Take the much-coveted Aeron chair from Herman Miller. The company introduced this puffy, bouncy desk chair for star executives and invented a market where none had previously existed. Suddenly, you could spend a lot of money on a chair that actually worked better, as opposed to just one that made you look bigger when you were busy firing people. When Internet marketing pioneer Site Specific raised its first round of venture capital, the principals went out and spent $15,000 on these chairs! This is a chair so remarkable, it was featured on the front page of the *Wall Street Journal.*

Now, of course, there are plenty of neat, ergonomic desk chairs. One of Herman Miller's biggest competitors is betting the farm on their new Leap chair. Their MBAs have taken a hard look at Aeron's success and market share and decided that they can capture x% of the market. The problem, of course, is that there's no longer a vacuum. The problem is that now, instead of spreading a virus about how you can be more comfortable all day, they have to spread a much smaller, and less compelling virus about why their chair is a little better than the chair you've already heard of.

There are vacuums in your industry. But not for long. . . .

Once It Does Spread, An Ideavirus Follows A Lifecycle. Ignore The Lifecycle And The Ideavirus Dies Out. Feed It Properly And You Can Ride It For A Long Time.

Tom Peters co-wrote *In Search of Excellence* nearly twenty years ago. Through some smart marketing moves (not to mention a great virus) the book became an epidemic and turned into the bestselling business book ever written.

Tom's career could have followed the arc of almost every other business writer . . . a big hit followed by a long decline into obscurity. But instead of ignoring the lifecycle, Tom insisted on riding it.

And he's still riding it today. Every few years he unleashes a new ideavirus. He writes mindblowing articles (like the "Brand Called You" cover piece for *Fast Company* a few years ago) and follows up with books and exhausting worldwide speaking tours. When he shows up in a town to give a speech, perhaps a third of the people there are dyed-in-the-wool Tom Peters fans. And the rest of the audience? Brought there by the fans, exposed to his virus, ready to be turned into fans.

By leveraging the base that his first book brought him, Tom has built a career out of launching new ideaviruses. Sure, none of them were as big as *In Search of Excellence,* but the vacuum keeps getting smaller, so the opportunities are smaller.

Other companies and ideas have ridden their first wave and then disappeared. People no longer clamor to do the Hustle or to get into Studio 54. They don't visit the once hot jennicam website or pay a premium for front row seats at *Cats.* Why? Because instead of institutionalizing the process of improving, honing and launching new ideaviruses to replace the dying ones, the "owners" of these viruses milked them until they died.

Viral Marketing Is An Ideavirus, But Not All Ideaviruses Are Viral Marketing.

Viral marketing is a special case of an ideavirus. Viral marketing is an ideavirus in which the medium of the virus *is* the product. It's an idea where the idea *is* the amplifier.

Steve Jurvetson, the venture capitalist behind Hotmail, coined the term "viral marketing" to describe the way the

DEFINITION: AMPLIFIER A key difference between word of mouth and an ideavirus is that word of mouth dies out while an ideavirus gets bigger. Why? Because something amplifies the recommendations to a far larger audience. That could be TV or other forms of media (a good review in the *New York Times* that amplifies the message of one reviewer to many readers) or it could be the web (a site like planetfeedback.com amplifies the message of a single user).

service grew. Hotmail offered free email. That alone was a very compelling two-word business proposition. But the magic of the company was that in every single email you sent using the service, there was a little ad on the bottom of the note. And the ad said, "Get Your Private, Free Email from Hotmail at www.hotmail.com."

Every time you sent a note, you spread the virus. The magic of viral marketing is that the product carries the message. The more you use Hotmail, the more you spread the virus. But note: It was also extremely smooth. The Hotmail site was just a click away from an email, and it took just a few clicks more to start using it—and to send Hotmail's built-in ads to *your* friends.

Unfortunately, not every product lends itself to viral marketing. Viral marketing requires that the product you're using be communications-focused or very public. The new VW Beetle is an example of viral marketing. Why? Because the more you drive it, the more people see it. And the more

Beetles people see, the more Beetles people want. It's not audible and it's not as smooth as Hotmail, but it is most definitely viral.

Many of the very best Internet ideas are built around some level of viral marketing. Using an earlier example, Referrals.com pays big money to people who recruit their friends for hot jobs. Of course, the act of recruiting your friends is also the act of telling them about Referrals.com.

Try not to get too obsessed with the magic, self-referencing nature of the best viral marketing senarios. They're a very special case—for example, it's hard to imagine how most books could use viral marketing. Interesting, though, that line-dances like the Hustle and the Macarena *did* benefit from viral marketing. After all, you can't do the dance unless you teach your friends how!

What Does It Take To Build And Spread An Ideavirus?

There are two questions you can ask yourself about your idea before you launch it, questions that will help you determine how likely your idea will become an ideavirus.

Is it worth it?

Nobody spreads an ideavirus as a favor to you. They do it because it's remarkable, thought-provoking, important, profitable, funny, horrible or beautiful. In today's winner-take-all world, there's no room for a me-too offering, or worse, *boring* products and services. If it's not compelling, it will never lead to an ideavirus.

Face it. Nobody is going to hand out big rewards ever
again for being on time, performing work of good quality,
being useful, finishing a project on budget or being *good
enough.* That's expected. That's a given. The rewards (and
the ideavirus) belong to the first, the fastest, the coolest,
the very best.

The biggest mistake companies make is that they chicken
out. If your idea doesn't become a virus, it's most likely because it didn't deserve to become a virus.

If you're now defining yourself as an idea merchant (hey,
it's either that or lose), then you must accept the fact that
being brave and bold in the creation of ideas is the only reason to go to work today.

Is it smooth?

After someone's been exposed to an ideavirus just once,
they're not likely to actually catch it. We've made our brains
bulletproof and ideaproof. There's so much clutter, so much
noise, so many ideas to choose from that the vast majority of
them fail to make a dent.

Think about the last time you walked through a bookstore (the home of ideaviruses waiting to happen). How
many books did you stop and look at? Pick up? Turn over?
And how many of those books ended up in your shopping
basket? Got read? Led you to tell ten friends? Precious few,
that's for sure.

Compare this to the Harry Potter phenomenon.
The bestselling books of the last few years became an
ideavirus when kids told kids. A classic ideavirus, and one

that initially grew with no promotion at all from the publisher.

It's difficult to get from awareness to the "sale" of an idea, to convert a stranger into a friend and a friend into a carrier of your ideavirus. An ideavirus succeeds when it pierces our natural defenses and makes an impact.

In Greek mythology, Medusa was the most famous of the race of Gorgons—beings with a horrible curse. Anyone who looked in their eyes immediately and permanently turned to stone.

There are plenty of marketers who wish that their ads or their product had the power of Medusa: that every person who saw the ad would be immediately transfixed, rooted to the spot, and converted into a customer for life. (Of course, they don't want their customers to die a horrible death and be turned into stone, but I couldn't find a Greek myth in which an evil goddess turned you into a frequent shopper of Kate Spade purses, getting a second mortgage just to pay for the habit.)

Alas, there are precious few Gorgon products and even fewer ad campaigns with Gorgon-like properties. It's foolish to expect that one exposure to your message will instantly convert someone from stranger to raving ideavirus-spreading fan. So plan on a process. Plan on a method that takes people from where they are to where you want them to go.

And while you're at it, work on the product. Because a catchier, more compelling, more viral product makes your job 100 times easier.

These are critical decisions because of the attention deficit marketers are facing. In 1986, the year I published my first book, there were about 300 other business books published. In 1998, there were 1,778 business books brought to market.

The supermarket sees about 15,000 new products introduced every year. The Levenger catalog alone features more than 50 different pens and pencils, none of which were available just a couple years ago. There isn't a marketplace out there that isn't more crowded than it was a decade ago.

In a world where products are screaming for attention, the most precious commodity is attention. And attention is harder and harder to achieve.

If you already understand the power of permission, your next question might be, "Fine, but how do we get permission? How do we get the first date . . . the first interaction where we ask people if we can start an ongoing dialogue about our products and their needs?"

My answer used to be a rather weak mumble about buying ads. The right answer, however, is to create an ideavirus. The right answer is to let the market tell itself about your products and services and give you permission to continue the dialogue without your having to pay for it each time. The right answer is to create products so dynamic and virusworthy that you *earn* the attention.

There Are Three Key Levers That Determine How Your Ideavirus Will Spread.

Where do you start? What are the key elements worth focusing on to turbocharge your idea and turn it into a virus? There are three things to focus on:

1. How big do you launch?
2. How smooth is it?
3. How can you turn trial into persistence?

1. How many people know about it before the spreading starts?

You can launch big or you can launch small. Vindigo (a viral phenomenon discussed in detail later) launched their Palm ideavirus with just 100 people. Within weeks, that number had grown to 3,000, and then quickly to more than 100,000. All without advertising. However, if you're entering a vacuum and there's plenty of competition on the horizon, launching big (while more expensive) can increase the chances that you'll succeed.

How to launch big? With traditional interruption advertising. With sponsorships. With free samples. One of the dumbest things marketers do is put artificial barriers in the way of trial. For example, it's obvious that one of the best ways to kill sales of a new car is to charge people $100 to take a test drive.

But charging for a test drive is just as dumb as a politician charging people to hear a speech, or a movie studio charging for the coming attractions. When you launch an ideavirus, the more people who can see it *fast,* the faster it will spread.

2. The importance of smoothness.

In addition to being persistent and cool, an ideavirus spreads the fastest when it's smooth. Persistence matters because the longer people are sneezing about your idea, the more people they infect. Cool is critical because if it's not virusworthy, it's just not going to take off. But smooth is essential because if you make it *easy* for the virus to spread, it's more likely to do so. In viral marketing (for products like the Polaroid camera and Ofoto.com) the ideal solution is to build smooth transference tools right into the idea—which can be difficult.

But that doesn't mean you shouldn't try. Amazon tried with "Member Get a Member" promotions, in which they

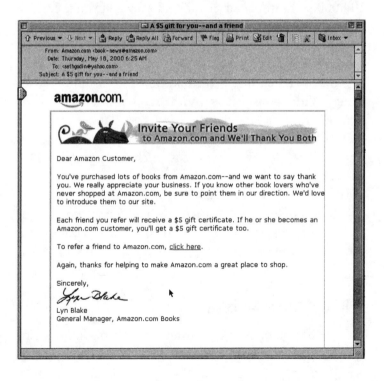

bribe members to tell their friends to buy books from Amazon (*get $5 for your friends and $5 for you!*). ZDNet puts a button next to every story they publish on their website: *click here to send this article to a friend.* Smooth.

Tupperware built an entire company around the smooth transfer of product enthusiasm from one friend to another. When you have a Tupperware party you are simultaneously hanging out with friends, demonstrating products you like, selling them *and* recruiting other people to do the same to their friends. By focusing obsessively on how to make it smooth, you can dramatically increase the velocity of the ideavirus.

3. Turning trial into persistence.

Sooner or later, you've got to turn momentary attention into an embrace of your idea, and then, hopefully, into conversion of the user into a sneezer.

Permission marketing becomes a critical tool in working people through this transition. The Hare Krishnas have grown their sect by inviting people to eat a vegetarian dinner with them. Intrigued or just hungry, people give them momentary attention and then permission to talk to them about this new way of life.

Sometimes people leave, having done nothing but eaten dinner. Sometimes, people listen to what's being said and decide to embrace the ideals being discussed. And sometimes, they become converted and turn into sneezers, volunteering to go out and invite *other* people over for dinner the next night.

Note that they didn't start by walking up to a stranger and proselytizing about their religion. Instead, they used a gradual technique to sell their idea effectively and turn it into a virus. Are there religions that are *not* viruses? Sure, the Shakers were almost anti-viral . They didn't try to convert in any of the usual, proactive ways. That's why there are so few Shakers left.

On the web, this multi-step process is too often overlooked by companies facing short-term financial pressure (combine this with the legendary short attention span of entrepreneurs and you can see why this happens). Instead of building a virusworthy cool product or service, identifying a hive, promoting an idea, and making it smooth and persistent, they just spend a few million dollars to buy advertising.

The hope, of course, is that somehow by spending enough money on clever ads, they'll magically create a critical mass of positive energy that will turn their idea into a virus. They're looking for a shortcut, and as a result, leading their companies to doom. Building a virus takes insight, talent and most of all, patience.

After a consumer is interested enough to visit ZDNet or Google.com or some other neat new site, what should these sites do to augment the ideavirus? Three things:

1. Get permission to follow up: make it easy for me to learn about *why* I should embrace this idea over time. All those ads you ran are a great way to get someone to your site, but it might cost your site $100 in marketing expenditures to get that one visit from just one consumer. If you don't get permission to follow up, the entire $100 is wasted.

2. Make as many supporting manifestos available as possible, in whatever forms necessary, to turn consumers from skeptics into converts. This can include endorsements, press reviews, even criticisms and common objections. Think of the Hare Krishnas at dinner. The more they can expose you to during that hour, the better their odds of spreading the virus.

3. Make it easy for consumers to spread the ideavirus by providing a multitude of tell-a-friend tools, as well as overt rewards for becoming a sneezer.

Thirteen Questions Ideavirus Marketers Want Answered

1. Have we chosen a hive we're capable of dominating?
2. How likely are the powerful sneezers to adopt our virus?
3. Do we know who the powerful sneezers are and how to contact them?
4. What can we do to our product to make it more virus-worthy?
5. Are we prepared to reward promiscuous sneezers sufficiently to get them on our side?
6. Have we figured out what we want the sneezers to say? How are we teaching them to say it?
7. Even if our product isn't purely viral by nature, is it possible to add more viral marketing elements to it (or to our marketing approach)?
8. Do we know how to get permission from people once they've been touched by the virus? Do we know what to say after we get permission?
9. How smooth is the transfer of the ideavirus?

10. Is our offering good enough to wow this hive?
11. Do we have the resources and time to dominate this hive before others rush in to fill the vacuum?
12. Have we built in multiple feedback loops so we can alter the virus as it moves and grows?
13. Have we identified the vector we want the virus to move in, and have we built the tools and plans to keep it moving in the vector we'd like?

Five Ways To Unleash An Ideavirus

The most important thing to remember when unleashing an ideavirus is that for best results *you must build this thinking in from the very beginning.* If you've got an existing product or service and you're hoping to build a virus around it, your job will be more difficult. The ideas behind the lightning fast success stories have all worked because the ideavirus concept was baked in from the start. That's one of the reasons more established companies are having so much trouble competing in the new economy—they're restricted because of the standards and systems they built in years ago.

The five techniques, in order of sheer market power, are:

1. Go full viral. The more you use it, the more you market it (whether you want to or not). In essence, using the product is the same as marketing it.
2. Pay off the promiscuous.
3. Make it smooth for the powerful.
4. Digitally augment word of mouth.
5. Altruism . . . reward the friends of the promiscuous.

1. Go full viral.

This is the holy grail of ideavirus marketing. The beauty of viral marketing is that if you properly construct the virus, you can grow like a weed and dominate the market—if you can do it before the competition.

Polaroid and Hotmail are the poster children for viral marketing, but there are a few others that are worth looking at:

Blue Mountain Arts was a pioneer in creating a virus around the idea of sending electronic greeting cards. The virus is simple to understand—in order to send a greeting card successfully, you've got to send it *to* someone. Of course, once someone receives the card, if they like the idea, they're just a click away from sending someone else a card!

Even though the cards featured by Blue Mountain Arts could charitably be called "cheesy," the virus caught on. People got the idea that it might be fun to send electronic cards to their friends . . . and the idea spread. The company started small, with no real advertising. Just a few people sent the first batch of cards.

But then the magic of viral marketing kicked in. Let's assume that each person sends cards to five people. Let's also assume that those recipients have a 50% chance of being interested enough in the concept to go to the site and send cards to five of *their* friends. If we start with ten people, the generations look like this:

10 people send 50 cards
which means that 25 people get the virus and send 125 cards

which means that 63 people get the virus and send 315 cards

which means that 162 people get the virus and send 810 cards

which means that 405 people get the virus and send 2025 cards . . .

Now, that may seem like a slow start, but if you assume that each generation takes three days to occur (I send out ten cards and within three days, five friends show up and do the same thing), then you'd have 58 million users in 54 days!

Of course, that doesn't really happen. It's unlikely you'll be able to continue to get a 50% conversion rate. And it's certain that you'll soon hit duplication, with individuals starting to get cards from different people. But the math is nevertheless stunning.

The key number in the equation is the percentage of people who convert. If you lower it from 50% in the Blue Mountain Arts example to 30%, the number of users drops from 58 million to less than 10,000. Which is why conversion is so critical.

The battle between Hallmark and Blue Mountain in this space is fascinating. Hallmark and American Greetings, both old-line card companies, were well aware of the potential of the Internet. But they were also unable to imagine a world in which cards didn't cost money—so they made the cards they sold online available for a fee.

As a result, no virus emerged from the Hallmark site. If someone was charmed by a card and came to the site to send a few, they discovered that they'd have to *pay* to do that.

They didn't convert. Conversion fell below the *magic number* and the virus never ignited.

You can compute the magic number by multiplying the number of cards the average user sends (in the example above, it's 5) by the percentage of people who convert (50%). In this case, the magic number is 2.5, which is how much bigger each generation will be than the one before. Until the magic number exceeds 1.2 or 1.3, it's hard for a product to get viral fast enough to beat the competition.

By focusing on smoothness (it's only three clicks to send a card and it's free, so go ahead and try it), Blue Mountain built an amazing conversion machine. As a result, the site grew and grew until Excite bought it for nearly a billion dollars worth of stock. Whatever Blue Mountain's goal—to make a lot of money, to affect a lot of people or to spread their idea far and wide—they've succeeded.

Hallmark and American Greetings have seen the light, and now they, along with Yahoo! and others, offer free greeting cards. The challenge that they face is that there's no longer a vacuum, so their ideavirus can't spread as fast, and their magic number is far lower than that which Blue Mountain Arts enjoyed at its peak (the number *must* go down as the population of untouched people approaches zero).

Another example of viral marketing worth looking at is Ofoto.com. Ofoto is an Internet alternative to Fotomat. Instead of dropping your film off at the corner, you send your digital camera files to Ofoto and they send back beautiful prints.

This is a compelling story, but there isn't enough money in the world to communicate it through traditional marketing means. Kodak spends $100 million a year in advertising (and has been advertising for a hundred years). On top of the huge amount of noise out there, there are just no easy media channels Ofoto can use to spread its message in a cost-effective, fast way to the target hive: digital photography users.

So Ofoto also launched a digital photo album. This album lets you post your favorite digital photos online, for free, and invite friends to come see them. Here's the good part: a digital photo album with no one looking at it is worthless!

Thus, once you upload your photos, you've got to motivate your friends and relatives to stop by and see the photos. You become Ofoto's #1 marketing weapon.

Take pictures of your kid's soccer team. Upload them. Tell everyone on the team where to find the photos.

Some of the parents will like the photos so much they'll click a button and buy a print. Ofoto has a new customer. Interestingly, the content was created by someone else—not the person who bought the photo. This is an effect that never happens to Kodak.

Even better, some people who see the photos of the soccer team will realize that they too would like to be able to post pictures for friends. So the torch passes, and Ofoto has added another photographer to its ever growing stable.

It's worth noting that the conversion rate for Ofoto is almost certainly going to be lower than it was for Blue Mountain Arts, because it's much less smooth. In order to spread the word that you've posted someone's picture, you've got to find that person and tell them about it, and then they've got to hustle themselves to a computer to look at it . . . not as clean as the all-electronic approach of Blue Mountain.

If I want to buy a print, I've got to enter my name and address, *and* I've got to pay for it. If I want to upload photos, I've got to figure out how to use my digital camera upload files, or I've got to mail in my traditional film to Ofoto for developing.

Despite these obstacles, Ofoto has a very positive magic number as demonstrated by the fact that they've amassed more than 500,000 users in less than 12 weeks.

The astute reader has probably noticed a critical difference between Hotmail and Blue Mountain Arts vs. Ofoto.

Hotmail and Blue Mountain Arts are self-referencing ideaviruses. The virus spreads with the use of the product *whether the user wants it to or not.* When you first start using Hotmail, the self-promoting signature line promoting Hotmail is automatically included in every email you send. You didn't choose to do that (though you can turn it off), it just goes along anyway.

In the case of Blue Mountain, the symbiotic relationship between the product and the marketing is even more obvious. The card *is* the marketing, so using it is, by definition, promoting it.

Ofoto, on the other hand, does no such thing. You could quite happily use Ofoto for developing, sorting and storing your photos and never recommend it to anyone.

Clearly, if the marketing element is benign and totally integrated into your offering, your magic number is going to be much higher; the symbiosis pays off with big dividends. The product has 100% efficiency, and every user becomes a promoter. The challenge is this: it only works for a very select group of products and services—probably not yours.

Why have I gone to great lengths to point out that viral marketing is merely a subset of ideavirus marketing? Because while very few of us will ever be lucky enough to enjoy the full fruits of a viral marketing campaign, most of us *can* unleash an ideavirus.

2. Pay off the promiscuous.

Paying powerful sneezers in an effort to make them promiscuous (but have them keep their power) is an extremely difficult balancing act, but if you do it successfully, you can turn it into a billion dollar business.

Some people call it network marketing or multi-level marketing. Others think of it as a paid celebrity endorsement. But it can be as simple as member-get-a-member for your local health club.

The basic idea is simple: If your recommendation is going to help my business, I'm happy to pay you to recommend me.

The implementations vary all over the map. When Nike paid the coach of the Duke University basketball team millions of dollars (for him, not Duke) to coerce his team members to switch to Nike shoes, they were turning a formerly powerful sneezer into a promiscuous one. Why? When people see what the Blue Devils wear, they might decide to wear the same thing.

On the Net, technology makes it easy to take this model and make it much more personal. Amazon's affiliate program, in which Amazon pays users a portion of the book revenue they generate through referrals, is built around this model.

Go to www.permission.com. There, at the bottom of the page, is a link where you can buy a copy of *Permission Marketing*. Click on it and it will take you to Barnes & Noble or Amazon—right to the page on the site that sells *Permission Marketing*. Both stores give me a kickback on every sale.

Did I send you to Amazon *just* because I'm going to get a kickback? Nope. It doesn't do me any good to recommend a bookseller where you won't end up buying the book—I'll end up with no kickback and no book sales either. I recommended Amazon because you're likely to have one-click shopping already set up, increasing the chances the book will get sold. I also recommended Barnes & Noble, because their affiliate program is at least as good, and some of my readers would prefer to shop there. But the kickback still influenced my decision, and has clearly motivated hundreds of thousands of individuals and businesses to set up links to their favorite books at Amazon and at Barnes & Noble.

This approach is far less risky than Nike's. Nike has no idea if the Blue Devils actually sell shoes. They also have to pay for the endorsement in advance, with no refunds if they're wrong.

Amazon and other affiliate marketers, on the other hand, are using the power of the Net to create a deal with no losers and no downside. You can set up an affiliate link in a few minutes. For free. If it works, you get paid. If it doesn't work, you don't. And it doesn't cost Amazon a dime.

Because of this risk model, affiliate programs are flourishing. BeFree.com, a leading provider of services to marketers using this approach, calls it Performance Marketing. They currently list 235 websites that are offering affiliate programs.

While it may be interesting to earn a dollar or two on a sale (interesting, that is, if you can sell thousands a month), some companies are taking a different tack.

Woody Chin, founder of Referrals.com, thinks he's found a way to change the way people interact when it comes to job hunts and other sorts of business-to-business commerce. Instead of paying people a nickel or even a buck, he's paying people $1,000 to $5,000 *each* for that priceless commodity: a referral.

Here's how job filling worked before Referrals.com: Hire a contingency headhunter. Offer to pay a third of the final salary, but only if you hire someone the headhunter brings along. So the hunter stands to earn $20,000 or more.

Now, the headhunter hits the phones. She calls everyone she can, and basically begs for leads. There's no obvious benefit to the referrer, except for the possible goodwill that occurs when you find a friend a job. Woody and Referrals.com are aiming to change that.

With Referrals.com, the hiring manager sends out a description of the job to people she thinks might know good candidates. These referrers can be people she knows in the industry, company insiders or super-agents (and anyone can be a super-agent—read on). The key here is that the referrals are from people whose opinions she values. The description includes a bounty she is willing to pay for a hire as well as a limit to how deep and how wide a referral tree she desires.

It's fascinating to see that Referrals.com is building in a *limit* to the ideavirus! They don't want any given job search to get out of control and start being passed from friend to friend ad infinitum. Instead, they artificially limit how deep a job search can go into the community. This limit ensures that employers can focus their searches on a certain hive without it running amok throughout the entire population. The web has turned what might have been a multi-level marketing business into a carefully regulated ideavirus.

Anyone who gets involved in referring can sign-up to be a "super-agent." Once you sign up as a super-agent, your performance ratings will be available to hiring managers (in recruiting) looking to find experts to help with their search. And of course, you get first crack at the new job listings.

Let's say the company wants a CTO. Let's say they're willing to pay $5,000 for a successful hire. And let's say they're only willing to go two levels down the referral tree.

Now, a super-agent can send an email to five people he knows who might be perfect for the job. If one of them takes the job, the super-agent gets $5,000 just for sending five emails.

But let's say none of the recipients want the job. But one of them knows someone who does. Bang. He forwards the mail a second time, and this time it lands on the desk of the perfect hire. Assuming this guy gets the job, the first super-agent and the second referrer split the money.

All of a sudden, you've monetized word of mouth! Referrals.com could create a class of thousands of super-agents who spend their time doing nothing but finding people through networking. Essentially, it lets just about anyone become a contingency headhunter. (Now, I know what you think of contingency headhunters . . . but the small scale of each person's tree makes it unlikely it'll ever get that bad!)

Of course, it goes deeper than this. If it works for head-hunting, maybe it works for finding new clients for Viant, or for people who are looking to take a cruise. Or what about real estate? If everyone could become a contingency broker, doesn't life online get interesting? If the Internet succeeds when it monetizes previously random analog events (like garage sales at eBay) then this may just be the killer app for this space.

Does Referrals.com work? I have no idea. It's just launching. We don't know if the promiscuous will overwhelm the powerful and pollute the whole system. We don't know the velocity of the idea or how long this particular virus will last. But it's clear that *something* will replace the current model of headhunters spamming powerful sneezers and essentially stealing their rolodexes.

Alladvantage.com wanted to take the multi-level marketing approach instead. Each person they signed up got a commission on the revenue generated by the people *those* people signed up. And so on.

They got off to a very hot start, signing up millions of users in a very short period of time. But now, according to the *Wall Street Journal,* they've discovered that maybe they were paying these promiscuous sneezers too much to make any money in the end. So Alladvantage just announced new rules in the way they pay their sneezers.

The result was predictable. Their most important sneezers were outraged. When you pay people to refer on your behalf, you've got to expect that they are indeed motivated by money, and when the money goes, so will your sneezers.

Multi-level marketing has gotten a bad reputation among powerful sneezers. Why? Because individuals are encouraged to suspend their judgment and embrace the idea that several generations down the pike, they'll be rich.

While this is a fine choice for an individual to make, it's problematic for those who are friends with this individual. Why? Because the personal interaction is no longer on a level playing field. Person A uses his friendship with person B to encourage her to buy or use something that isn't necessarily in her best interest. If she agrees, then person A sees a significant return, while person B inevitably sees LESS of a return. If she resists, the friendship is strained.

If the pyramid is steep enough (if there's enough money promised at the end of the tunnel), this sort of approach can work. But it usually leaves scorched earth in its path, and disappointments in the form of broken friendships or financial promises not met.

To date, very few companies—online or off—have figured out a way to turn network or multi-level marketing into a large, sustainable business. Those that have, like Rexall, Amway and perhaps Alladvantage, now have to work even harder to undo the bad reputation that this approach has earned.

3. Make it smooth for the powerful.

One of the most elegant ways to take advantage of the new tight networking among consumers is to identify the powerful members of a hive and make it as easy as possible for them to tell each other about an ideavirus.

When online content sites first debuted, they were extremely hesitant about sharing their articles. Some of them went so far as to make it impossible to copy and paste the text in an article. They were petrified that one person would copy an article and no one else would come to the site and see the ads.

What they soon learned, however, was that the easier they made it to share, the more likely people were to tell their friends. And if someone came in to read one article, they were likely to read more. ZDNet.com was one of the first sites I encountered that used this technique. In one promotion my former company, Yoyodyne, did for them, they found that more than 20% of the people exposed to a compelling piece of content actually forwarded it to a friend.

Fast Company magazine—devoted to bootstrapping start-ups—does the same thing. Visit www.fastcompany.com /team/wtaylor.html and you can see a list of the articles that co-founder Bill Taylor has written for that magazine. They're all there, unabridged, and you can read them for free.

But the smooth part of this wannabe ideavirus is the little button on the bottom that says "Click here to send this page to a friend." All you have to do is type in their email address and your email address and—boom—it's done. If his articles contain ideas that are virusworthy, the *Fast Company* site is doing a good job in helping them go viral.

Inside.com, which sells subscriptions to its online media newsletter and website for $200, is happy to have people send these pricey articles to non-subscribing friends. In fact, there's a big "send to a friend" button on the bottom of every article. The reason is obvious. Once you've read one, you might be willing to pay for more. All they need is a few of the ideas they publish to become viral and suddenly the business of selling subscriptions will get a lot healthier.

In essence, Inside.com is hoping that its readers will market the site for them, spreading ideas that might go viral and then bringing in new paying customers as a result.

4. Digitally augment word of mouth.

This is a really interesting way of looking at the fundamental change that's occurring, and understanding how word of mouth is different from an ideavirus.

If I was delighted by a movie in the old days, I'd tell a friend or two. My comments would end up influencing three or four or six people.

There are plenty of books on this topic and marketers have always been enamored by the potential of word of mouth. Alas, without amplification, it usually peters out.

Today, if I like a movie, I can post my comments on a variety of online movie sites. Or I can email ten friends (who can each forward the mail to ten friends). Later, when the video comes out, I can post my review on Amazon, where hundreds or thousands of people might read it.

Using a service like Epinions.com, I can go online and search out opinions on everything from BMW motorcycles to summer camps.

What's neat about digital word of mouth (let's call it word of mouse) is:

- It is extremely persistent. Unlike a comment at the water-cooler or over the phone, a comment in a newsgroup, on Epinions or Amazon lasts forever.
- It has much greater velocity. The number of ripples my stone makes when dropped in the pond of public opinion is far greater online. Why? Because if I tell you I like my car, it might be months before that sort of car comes up again in conversation. But online, conversations are happening 24 hours a day, and the "conversation" on any given web page is precisely about what that page is about. As a result, the number of interactions multiplies geometrically.
- It can have more credibility. At first, the opposite was true. An anonymous stock tip or other form of online recommendation was totally suspect. The sneezer could be a paid mole, or worse, someone with horrible taste. But now, thanks to rating systems and the presence of powerful sneezers, it's possible to know how congruent your tastes are with those of the sneezer, so it ends up having a ton of credibility.

Amazon is now rating the reviewers! A visit to www .amazon.com/exec/obidos/tg/cm/member-reviews/- /AFVQZQ8PW0L/102-7235345-2994554 shows me that Harriet Klausner is the top ranked reviewer on the entire site. Harriet, a retired librarian, has written more than 500 reviews and has received more than 5,000 votes from other folks who agree with her taste. If Harriet likes a book that you like, you're certainly going to give her sneeze some credence in the future.

5. Altruism.

Several years ago, a hot chef in Chicago decided to go out on his own and open his first restaurant. Realizing how competitive the market was, he did a neat thing. He never opened it to the public. He refused to accept reservations from strangers.

If you wanted to get into Les Nomades, you had to be a member. And how did you do that? Well, the first 500 people were given memberships because the chef knew them as regular customers at his old job, and he personally invited them.

Then he told each member that they were welcome to sponsor other members. All they had to do was vouch for someone and he'd make them a member too.

So, what's in it for the member to nominate someone else? Simple. They scored points with their friends as powerful sneezers because they could "get you in" to the hottest restaurant in town.

Of course, this wouldn't have worked if the restaurant hadn't been spectacular. But it was. And it was exclusive. But by allowing his members to do his marketing for him, by giving them an altruistic tool that increased their power as professional sneezers, the chef was able to get out of the way and let his customers sell for him.

THE IDEAVIRUS FORMULA

Managing Digitally-Augmented Word Of Mouth

That's what I would have called this book if it had been published by the Harvard Business Review. And you probably wouldn't be reading it now! Words matter. Understanding exactly what we're talking about makes it easier to do something about the world around us. That's why I take such great pains to invent new words and get us all thinking about exactly what they mean.

If we bump into each other at some convention and you ask me to talk about your business, I'll instantly start using words like hive and sneezer and velocity and smoothness. Why? Because these shorthand phrases make it easy for us to communicate. By using words that indicate we both understand the underlying factors that leverage an ideavirus, we're likelier to get something done.

The ideavirus formula has eight co-efficients. Each one represents not just a concept, but a variable that you can tweak to make your product or service more viral, to create the elements you need to drive your idea into the community.

Tweak The Formula And Make It Work

It may be possible to write down the key elements of building and spreading a virus as a mathematical formula. No, I don't think you'll use it. But understanding the co-efficients makes it easier to see what's important and what's not. They also help you see the wide range of factors that can help an idea go viral; focusing on the most highly leveraged factor for *your* idea is a first step in launching the virus.

Multiply these five factors:

[reputation benefit to powerful sneezer of recommending virus]

[selfish benefit to promiscuous sneezer of recommending virus]

[smoothness of sharing the virus with a friend]

[power of the amplifier used to spread positive word of mouth]

[frequency of interactions among hive members]

Divide by the sum of these two factors:

[number of times you need to expose someone in this hive in order for the virus to catch]

[number of different sneezers who have to recommend a
virus to a given individual for it to ignite]

And then multiply that by the product of these four factors:

[percentage of infected hive members likely to sneeze]
[number of people the infected sneezer is likely to con-
tact]
[persistence of the virus (how long does a sneezer sneeze?)]
[number of people infected/(divided by) number of people in the hive]

Comments on each component:

[reputation benefit to powerful sneezer of recommending
virus]

Powerful sneezers can't be bought. But don't forget that
they *are* selfishly motivated. Will this make me look smart?
Will it make someone else happy? Will it make the world a
better place? There are plenty of levers that motivate powerful sneezers to spread the word, and they are often complicated and subtle. Some of our favorite powerful
sneezers: Zagats, Linus Torvald, Paul Newman, Ruth Re-
ichl, Randall Rothenberg, Andy Hertzfeld, Chuck Close,
Spike Lee, Bill Taylor, Don Peppers, Peter Mayle, Alan
Greenspan and Yo-Yo Ma. You may not know all of these
names, and there are plenty of hive-based sneezers I've
never heard of, but what they all have in common is that

they're perceived as insightful and altruistic. Once people think they can be bought off, their power plummets.

[selfish benefit to promiscuous sneezer of recommending virus]

As we saw in the Amazon affiliate example, if you can make the benefit to the individual both significant and easy to achieve, people will respond to it. Amazon signed up hundreds of thousands of affiliates with a simple offer (get a percentage kickback on everything you recommend) and backed it up with a two-minute procedure for qualifying and actually getting started.

[smoothness of sharing the virus with a friend]

Once I want to tell someone about your idea, how do I do it? If it's got a dumb, hard-to-say name, or an embarrassing implication, I'll probably pass. On the other hand, Hotmail is smooth indeed, because every time I send email I'm talking about the idea.

The Polaroid camera used this smoothness brilliantly. After all, the only reason to take a picture is to show it to other people, and if you can make the showing (and the waiting) turn into a discussion of the idea, so much the better.

The beauty of Vindigo is similar. In order to tell you about Vindigo, I'm going to pull my Palm out of my pocket and show it to you. But once I show Vindigo to you, I'm only one button away from actually *giving* it to you. The thing I want to show you is how easy it is to give you, so the virus self-reinforces.

Ideally, you'll figure out not only what a sneezer should say to someone when they talk about your idea, you'll also make it easy and automatic for them to do so.

[power of the amplifier used to spread positive word of mouth]

The mother of a friend of mine was runner up for Miss America in the early 1960s. I think she lost to Anita Bryant. Alas, coming in second did very little for her career. Anita, on the other hand, made her fortune squeezing oranges. Point is that once she conquered that hive of a few judges, the news was amplified far and wide. And the amplification (as per Zipf's law) gave her the foundation to create a career.

A challenge in tailoring your ideavirus is to make sure that when you do conquer an individual or dominate a hive, the good news is amplified as far as possible, preferably at no cost to you.

[frequency of interactions among hive members]

Some hives (like teenage girls) interact with each other far more frequently (and with much more intensity) than others—like senior citizens. By understanding the frequency of hive interaction and then trying to focus on moments of high interactivity, you can dramatically increase the velocity of a virus.

Trade shows, for example, bring sneezers together for intense periods of information exchange. By doing something as simple as handing out hats with your logo on them, you make it more likely that you'll reinforce your message during this critical time.

[number of times you need to expose someone in this hive in order for the virus to catch]

Some viruses are smooth indeed. See them once and you understand them. It only took one exposure to the Macarena to get it. In general, the simpler the idea and the lower the risk, the more likely someone is to get infected. Most of all, though, this variable is driven by how viral the idea is to begin with. Meaning: is it cool, wonderful, important, dramatically better and fun?

[number of different sneezers who have to recommend a virus for it to ignite]

Not all ideas have Medusa qualities. We usually need to hear from external sources before we're willing to buy into the new thing, especially for risky ideas. Bestseller lists for books and other products are terrific, as are the sort of seal-of-approval validations that institutional sneezers look for. "Hey, if it's good enough for IBM . . ." say the more timid prospects.

Bestseller lists are a stand-in for the number of recommendations you need to decide. A bestseller list says, "There are 24,000 other people who liked this idea." The reviews on Amazon are another great example of this. When 50 people post a positive review, it counts for something.

The alternative, which also works, is actually hearing from sneezers one by one. Some ideas need only one sneezer to get you to try it (like a restaurant) while others might need a hundred (like switching over to using email or a Palm to run your business).

[percentage of infected hive members likely to sneeze]

Some hives are filled with sneezers. And some ideas make people sneeze more than others. When John McCain tried to capture his party's presidential nomination, he discovered an entire population of people, previously dormant, who were so moved by his candor and campaign finance message that they started sneezing on his behalf. Not accidentally, many of these sneezers were in the media, carrying his message far and wide.

Another variable is your ability to increase the likelihood that people who don't usually sneeze decide that they'll make an exception just for you. Focus on the time and place of your introduction to the hive. Want your employees to spread an important new idea among themselves? Don't introduce it at the Friday afternoon beer blast, but rather make it a special event. Give them the tools they need to spread the word. Reward them for doing so, or make it clear how the virus will dramatically help your company. It's not an afterthought—it's the core of your marketing campaign.

[number of people the infected sneezer is likely to contact]

This is an especially important metric for promiscuous sneezers. Once you've converted people into spreading your message for their own personal gain, how can you incentivize them to spread the word to a *lot* of their friends? One way to do this is by offering increasing returns to the sneezer—the more you bring us, the more we give you (but be careful not to turn sneezers into spammers, who end up proselytizing strangers and causing a backlash). Referrals.com aims to do this by turning their best sneezers into super-agents, giving them better information and more money.

The same reasoning is obviously a factor in choosing which members of the media to contact. Saul Hansell at the *New York Times* has far more reach and influence than Jason Snaggs at the *Phoenix Register.* Seems obvious, but what most marketers miss is the fact that a very small number of powerful sneezers can have an impact outside their perceived influence. A reporter with the *right* readers could have far more sway over your virus than someone with plenty of reach but little influence.

[persistence of the virus (how long does a sneezer sneeze?)]

A short-lived experience that leaves no lasting effects is hard to turn into a virus, especially if it's not a social event like pop music (does every generation after ours realize just how bad their pop tunes are?). Tattoos, on the other hand, are extraordinarily persistent, so even though they're not very smooth, they continue to market themselves to other people for decades, making up what they lack in impact with sheer stick-to-it-ness.

[number of people infected /(divided by) number of people in the hive]

This is about measuring hive dominance. If just a small percentage of people in your chosen hive have been infected, you really have your work cut out for you. While you shouldn't compromise the essence of your idea in order to get a wide platform, you should be super-wary that you don't start with too small a sample of too large a hive. It's very easy for your virus to fade before it catches on.

Advanced Riffs On The Eight Variables You Can Tweak In Building Your Virus

In this section, we'll take a look at each of the eight underlying variables in the ideavirus formula, and try to get a handle on exactly how you can manipulate them for your product.

No two industries rely on the eight fundamental principles in precisely the same way. But virtually every ideavirus I've ever seen uses some of these principles in an extraordinary way, and just about every one could be improved if it expanded further into the other areas.

The Eight:

1. Sneezers
2. Hive

3. Velocity
4. Vector

5. Medium   7. Persistence
6. Smoothness   8. Amplifier

Sneezers

As described earlier, there are two kinds of sneezers: Powerful and Promiscuous. While all eight elements of the formula are critical, this is the area where many brand marketers have the most control, and thus the most influence.

Choose your sneezers—don't let them choose you. By focusing obsessively on *who* you're choosing to sneeze on your behalf, you build the foundation for your virus.

Powerful sneezers are certainly the most seductive, in that the right word from the right sneezer can make all the difference to your virus. If David Letterman visits your diner on television, or the *New Yorker* writes a twenty-page rave about your website, or if you win a MacArthur Fellowship grant, well, you've really made it.

Oprah Winfrey is quite possibly the most successful sneezer of our generation. She has single-handedly turned more than a dozen books into national bestsellers. She has launched a magazine that already has more than half a million subscribers. She can influence millions of the most powerful consumers in America, just by uttering a few sentences.

It's interesting to see how effectively Oprah and Martha Stewart have successfully monetized their position as powerful sneezers. If they trip and get perceived as promiscuous sneezers, as sneezers for hire, their effectiveness is quite reduced. But if they can maintain their position at the same time they sell books and magazines or sheets and towels, they've effectively leveraged their fame.

But few of us are that lucky. Most times, you're going to have to focus on powerful but less influential sneezers—individuals or organizations that have something to gain by endorsing your idea but aren't so out there that they're tagged as promiscuous sneezers.

Some powerful sneezers are very prominent and thus very hard to reach. The challenge for most marketers is to find the second tier of sneezer—the approachable, interested sneezer who can do almost as much for you as Oprah or Martha, but with whom you have a far greater chance of making an impact.

The story of *The Bridges of Madison County* is a great example of this. Warner Books, the publisher, realized that most other publishers were doing very little to market to the independent bookstores. If Warner could court the independents and give them something to sell that made them feel special, it would translate into a bestseller.

Of course, as soon as the legions of independent booksellers succeeded in turning *Bridges* into a phenomenon, they were assaulted by dozens of other less imaginative publishers, all trying to rush in and use the same strategy. Too late. It got cluttered. They got busy. No o ne else ever repeated the focused, obvious success of this approach.

Remember, an ideavirus adores a vacuum, and *Bridges* filled that vacuum. As other book marketers rushed in, no one was able ever again to persuade a critical mass of booksellers to support just one book to such a dramatic extent.

Does this mean Warner was doomed never to be able to repeat this process again? Is that all there is—just one new gimmick after another? No! Instead, Warner needed to gain permission from this critical sneezer audience and use that permission to promote the next book and the next through a channel they were clever enough to build.

Hive

Winning with an ideavirus begins with the choice of hive. And this choice is so important, I'd suggest the following: choose your hive first, *then* build the idea.

Traditionally, marketers start with a problem, or a factory, and go from there. I've got a great widget, and now I need a way to take it to market. Or, we've got this excess plant capacity—let's find a way to fill it. But that's not what works today. Choose your market by identifying a hive that has a problem *and* has the right concentration of sneezers, the right amplified networking, the right high velocity of communication and, most of all, an appropriate vacuum.

Success will come to marketers who attack small but intimate hives. Yes, Yahoo! and eBay hit huge home runs, but they're remarkable precisely because success across such a large hive is rare indeed. We can learn a more relevant lesson from magazines.

Fast Company is one of the fastest-growing (and most profitable) magazines ever. Why? Well it certainly helps that it's a great magazine. It also helps that the Internet created a huge demand for this sort of advertising space. But the real success came in the hive that the editors selected.

Turns out there are hundreds of thousands of people in mid-sized to large companies who are eager to do a great job, but feel frustrated at the slow pace and mind-numbing bureaucracy they face every day. Until *Fast Company*, the members of this hive didn't even know there were others just like them. They didn't have a tool they could use to reach their peers.

Fast Company became the identity, the bible, the badge of honor for this new hive. It gave them a way to communicate, to learn and to have confidence in themselves. By every measure, the magazine was virusworthy.

Just about every reader of *Fast Company* became a powerful sneezer. With no compensation and very little encouragement, they started signing up co-workers for subscriptions, Xeroxing page after page of the magazine and passing it around the office. The readers even created a worldwide network of support groups, meeting in cities on a monthly basis, with no help at all from the magazine.

Fast Company filled a vacuum. It got viral. It enchanted and connected with a huge legion of powerful sneezers. All because the editors chose the right hive and created a virusworthy product.

A few years later, Time Warner launched *Real Simple* magazine, inspired by the significant sales of books about simple living. So they launched a magazine dedicated to simplifying our lives. Obviously, it's aimed at a very different hive than that of *Fast Company*. Alas, the magazine is off to a slow start. Why?

Because this hive isn't the right one at the right time. Because there's a real lack of aggressive powerful sneezers.

Because the hive doesn't have a built-in forum for communicating with one another (it's not office-centric like *Fast Company*). As a result, the magazine is having a much harder time going viral.

Choosing your hive

The *Zagats Guide to New York City Restaurants* is a fascinating document. According to Zagats, the book is put together by 100,000 reviewers, who ate out an *average* of four times a week, spending an average of $40 a person. Do the math. That's more than $8,000 of mostly after-tax money spent on eating out every year.

This very special hive of people shares a demographic but is by no means typical of the U.S. population (which in itself is very different from the world at large). Trying to appeal to everyone is almost sure to fail, for the simple reason that everyone wants something different!

The reason there isn't one restaurant in Cincinnati or Indianapolis or Tallahassee that's as good as the Union Square Café in New York is not that the population can't afford the tab. There's certainly enough money in those towns to keep the seats filled in several restaurants of this ilk. It's simply that the hive that can afford these restaurants doesn't have a high velocity way to get the word out fast enough to keep the restaurateur happy. And it's not clear that they'd persist. In other words, eating in a New York-style fancy restaurant probably isn't the way these "out-of-town" hives choose to spend their time and money. Same thing's true for a New York hive that would not necessarily reward a French restaurant that might do just great in Paris. All of which is a very fancy way of saying, "If the hive doesn't want it, you picked the wrong hive."

Selecting a hive that respects the core value of your virus is a critical first step in laying the foundation for promoting the idea. College students want something different from gardeners, who are quite different from computer geeks. Targeting everyone is a sure path to failure.

Of course, the real reason you want to pick the right hive is not because their values match the benefits of your product. It's because when you pick the right hive (and a small enough hive) you have a chance of overwhelming it—of pumping so much positive juice into your digital word of mouth that you really do dominate, that so many sneezers are recommending you to the rest of the hive that the majority surrenders and the entire hive converts.

Once your idea starts coursing through a hive again and again and again, you'll have a piling on effect. People will want to be exposed to your idea just because everyone else in the hive they respect is talking about it.

The mistake that's so easy to make is to get greedy as you choose your hive, to say, "this product is for everyone" or "anyone can benefit from this idea." Well, there are seven billion people on the planet, so it's unlikely your comment is correct; even if it is, there's little chance that a virus would spread across a hive that big.

Far better to pick smaller hives and conquer them a few at a time. Far better to identify consumers when they're grouped in bunches (at a trade show, say, or geographically) and then allow the concentrated essence of your virus spread to other hives.

Coors did this with beer years ago. You could only get Coors in Colorado, then you could only get it west of the Mississippi. By concentrating their marketing dollars, they addressed a smaller hive. This enabled them to get a larger percentage of the hive to sample the product. This core group then had a smooth way to spread the word, and it quickly conquered one state after another.

Without any effort from the Coors people, the virus spread to the East Coast. Coors fielded thousands of requests from disappointed drinkers who wanted to try this beer they'd heard about, but couldn't.

Coors dominated a hive. Then they went national to try to fulfill the demand created when their hive spread the word. Unfortunately, the new hive was so large, it turned out to be difficult to satisfy and dominate.

Compare the powerful, nearly effortless spread of their idea with the challenges they face today. As a national brand in a stagnant market, growth by any method is hard to come by. They built their company on a unique virus, but they couldn't continue to grow their company the same way.

Velocity

Napster is a worldwide file sharing database that lets Internet users share MP3 files. In essence, you can listen to the digital record collection of millions of other people. The idea behind Napster turned into a virus and grew like crazy. Why?

They hit college campuses—a hotbed of communication. A virus can spread across a campus in a matter of hours.

When a dear friend of mine went to Tufts in the late 1970s his roommate started a rumor that Paul McCartney had died (this was before John Lennon's tragic death—they weren't *that* callous). Within an hour, they started hearing the rumor back—from friends of friends of friends who couldn't precisely remember where or how they'd heard it.

Napster was spread the same way. How? Because in addition to being on a college campus, Napster lives on the Internet. So, instead of being word of mouth as in the Paul McCartney example, it was digitally augmented word of mouth. On college campuses, everyone has email, and email is both instantaneous and amplified. You can send an email to thirty or forty friends as easily as you can write to one. So once a powerful sneezer had tried the software and confirmed that it worked as advertised, the word spread fast.

Why is velocity so important? Remember, filling a vacuum is far easier than going second. If the velocity of a virus isn't fast enough, a competitor may leapfrog past you into a new hive before you can get there, dominating as the "original" in that market.

This happened with beer, in which regional favorites have long survived the introduction of nationwide refrigerated delivery. It even happened with the college entrance exams, in which the ACT is favored in the Midwest, years after the SAT became the standard almost everywhere else in the world. The only reason this happened is that the ACT got to the Midwest first.

How does the Net change our economy so dramatically? Because it dramatically increases the velocity of viruses in various hives. Where it used to take weeks or months for a contractor to talk with suppliers before building an office tower, he can now do it in just a day using the Net.

This increase in velocity fundamentally changes the dynamic of a virus. Something newsworthy might have 20 or 30 or 100 cycles of communications before the issue itself becomes boring. In the days before the Net, if each cycle only touched one or two or three people, the virus would die before it got old. Today, these cycles allow the virus to mutate and evolve as it touches millions of people.

Vector

Richard Dawkins, a brilliant evolutionary theorist, had his own word for the phenomenon I'm calling ideaviruses: *memes*. He pointed out that a meme was like a living organism, surviving not in the real world, but in our world of ideas.

Like a real organism, memes could live and die, and more important, they could evolve. Every time a meme is passed from person to person, it gets touched, changed and—sometimes—improved.

Once a meme has been passed around enough, it ceases to evolve as quickly and just becomes a building block for future memes. Pop singers are experts at stringing together memes and turning them into concise snapshots of our lives. (Paul Simon is a favorite—Graceland, Kodachrome, the pop charts . . . you get the idea).

One of the behaviors noticed by Dawkins and practiced by anyone who markets with ideaviruses is that memes follow a vector. An idea doesn't spread evenly and nicely through a population. Instead, people are more likely to send it in one direction instead of another.

At college, there was always someone who knew where the good parties were (and which ones to avoid). In your town, there's someone who just seems to have the inside buzz on which restaurants are hot. On the Internet, some people seem to be on the vector of the latest email joke, while others—even in the same company or the same cliques—just don't seem to get touched as often.

When you create an idea and lay the groundwork for it to become a virus, it pays to study the vector you'd like it to follow. Why? Because there's plenty you can do to influence its vector, and the vector you choose will have a lot to do with who "gets" the virus. The vector controls the hives through which the idea flows.

If you're on the Net, for example, the barriers you erect will influence your vector. If your site needs Shockwave and Flash and a high-bandwidth connection, you're not likely to vector straight into the heart of the AOL user universe, regardless of where you start. If your goal is to create a trading card mania among third graders, launching a series of cards available only at liquor stores isn't going to enhance the vector, even if you seed the virus by handing the cards out at the local elementary school.

But this is about more than simple access. Remember, the goal is to market to people and then get out of the way. So an email joke (which almost anyone with a job in this country could access at home, at work or at the library) will still find its vector. How? There are three factors:

1. **Who it starts with.** Often, the way we decide which direction to send an idea is based on where it came from. It's hard, for example, to bring home a joke from the office. Instead, we're more likely to send it straight back into the quadrant of life from which it came.
2. **Who it resonates with.** An idea has to have impact to be worth sharing at all, and we're much more likely to share that idea with someone whom we believe it will impact as well. After all, if we spread ideas that don't go viral, it hurts our reputation as powerful sneezers. This encompasses the idea of access . . . I'm not likely to spread an idea if the recipient doesn't have the energy or the technology or the resources to get engaged with it.
3. **What's easy.** The medium drives the spread of ideas more than you might imagine. If I have to print something out, put it in an envelope and mail it to someone, that virus is going to stop right there. That's why TV and the Internet have proven to be such powerful media for the spread of viruses—they're easy.

Medium

Scientists wasted hundreds of years looking for the medium by which light traveled. They knew it was making it through the vacuum of space, through water and through air, but without a medium, they couldn't figure out how it worked.

The medium is probably the most overlooked part of ideavirus planning and construction. It's so obvious, we often don't see it.

In Japan, teenage schoolgirls started and built a craze to billion-dollar proportions. They continue to line up to use a special kind of photo booth. Here's how it works: You enter the photo booth (similar to the old Polaroid ones of our youth), insert some coins and it takes your picture. But, instead of giving you four shots on a strip, it prints out 16 little one-square-inch images on stickers.

Now, what are you going to do with 16 pictures of yourself on stickers? Obvious—share them with your friends! As a result, every popular Japanese schoolgirl has an autograph book loaded with dozens or hundreds of these stickers. Sort of like your high school yearbook signing ceremony, but on steroids.

A friend of mine, Sam Attenberg, developed and patented this technology in the States. And while it never became a full-fledged virus in the U.S., it did develop pockets of intense activity in certain hives. Some machines were turning $70 an hour in sticker business, every hour on the hour for weeks at a time. In Japan, two companies dominate a multi-billion-dollar industry in Sticker Stations.

So what's the medium? It's the person-to-person exchange of stickers. The medium is the key to the entire virus. Once the first person got the sheet of stickers, the only way she could use them was by sharing them with 15 friends. But in sharing them, in using the medium provided, she had to explain where she got them. Boom. Virus spreads.

PayPal.com is another example of an extremely virulent idea that spread because the medium was so powerful. PayPal.com is an online service that allows customers of eBay and other auction sites—to transfer money online safely and securely. Now, when you pay for something you buy on eBay, you can just PayPal.com your money to the person.

Here, the medium is the money. People care a lot about money, and since, in this case, it solves a time-consuming problem (sending checks and waiting for them to clear), it's particularly welcome. And, just as we saw in the Sticker Station example, the act of using the medium causes us to teach others about the idea.

In both cases, a focus on the medium led to the ultimate success of the virus.

Smoothness

The goal, of course, is to have an ideavirus so smooth that once someone is exposed to it, they are instantly hooked. A virus so powerful that all it takes is one guitar lick on the radio, one phrase in a book review, one glimpse of a website and you completely and totally "get it." And not only do you get it, but you want it. Now and forever.

One of the talents of the great Steve Jobs is that he knows how to design Medusa-like products. While every Macintosh model has had flaws (some more than others), most of them have had a sexiness and a design sensibility that has turned many consumers into instant converts. Macintosh owners upgrade far more often than most computer users for precisely this reason. We *have* to own that new flat panel display. We *must* have the new color of iBook.

Vindigo is Medusa-like in the way the virus spreads so smoothly. It only takes one look at a friend's Palm in order to get hooked (and one file beaming to get it forever). The

Nextel phone has that power, and so (for some people) does Britney Spears.

Alas, it's not going to happen for you. While you can aspire to make your product more Medusa-like, it's a mistake to spend all your time wishing for it to happen. The odds are long indeed, especially if your product is not groundbreaking. The longer it takes someone to get the basic concept behind your idea, the less Medusa-like it is. But often, that's a good thing. Real change, and the profit that goes with it, often comes from unsettling ideas that significantly alter the way people interact with each other and with your company. And those ideas aren't as smooth as some others.

Persistence

In our quest for the quick hit, the easy way to start a business or to increase our power as sneezers, there's a real desire for a shallow virus. A joke. A gimmick. A neat new technology geegaw that won't be around tomorrow.

Laser pointers are a fine example. I was in a meeting recently where the presenter used a laser pointer to highlight various things on his deathly boring Powerpoint slides. Unfortunately for me, not only was the presentation boring, but he kept aiming the laser at the TV monitor, which reflected this highly focused electromagnetic radiation right at my face, hitting me in the eye a few times. I finally got him to turn the thing off, but not without considerable struggle.

Other than this unfortunate incident, I can't remember how many years it has been since I saw someone actually using one of these pointers.

What happened was that the pointer came out, and for a few early adopters, it felt marvelous. It touched a Jungian need in us (especially men, I think) to have a magic stick that could project our thoughts on the wall. Of course, the best place to use one was in a meeting of other nerds. And all the other nerds noticed the laser pointer and a virus was spread.

But after we all went out and bought laser pointers, we discovered that they weren't particularly useful. After all, how much information could one really have to present that we needed a high-tech device to point out the good stuff from the bad?

So the lasers ended up in a drawer.

In other words, the virus wasn't persistent. Those who resisted the initial temptation to rush out and buy a laser pointer stopped being exposed to them, and the virus died off.

Compare this to the Palm virus. Every day, somebody else marches into your office, declaring their undying love and devotion to his new pocket wonder. And unlike laser pointers, people who love them keep using them. They persist.

In Gladwell's terms, the Palm has now tipped in certain hives. So many people are using it so often that you're constantly reminded that unless you get one, you're a loser. It's the persistence of the Palm more than any other viral factor that has led to its success.

Amplifier

Word of mouth by itself isn't enough. As discussed earlier, unamplified word of mouth dies off too soon to be much good to the average business. The goal of a marketer creating an ideavirus is to create a system that allows the positive word of mouth to be amplified (and the negative to be damped!).

This simple idea is behind the success of Planetfeedback.com. It's impossible for me to understand why any business invited by Planetfeedback to participate would hesitate for even a moment before signing up.

If a consumer has a complaint or a compliment about a company, she can go to Planetfeedback and turn it into a letter to the company. Then, with a click, she can have a copy of the email go to the relevant congressmen, media and regulatory agencies. Another click can send a copy of the letter to the consumer's ten closest friends and co-workers.

Instant amplification.

Now, if your company is the target of a complaint, which course of action makes sense? You could either proactively grab the opportunity to stamp out a negative virus, to turn the complainer from an angry reporter of bad news into a now-satisfied witness to how much your company cares, *or* you could ignore them and hope they'll go away. Of course, they won't go away. They—and the people already infected— will continue to amplify the message.

Planetfeedback is providing a great service to all parties involved. By taking previously invisible word of mouth and aggregating it, they're making it easier for companies to understand the viruses that are already being spread, and they're giving them an opportunity to do something about them. And yes, they are viruses—ideas that are running amok, being passed from person to person. At the same time, Planetfeedback gives consumers far more power, and makes it easier for them to get attention.

Of course, you don't have to sponsor Planetfeedback. Some day they may offer a different program . . . or your competitors can pay to talk to your unhappy customers instead of you.

SECTION 4

CASE STUDIES
AND RIFFS

The Vindigo Case Study

One of the best examples of a company unleashing an ideavirus is Vindigo. You can find them at vindigo.com

on the web, and you'll need a Palm (or something compatible) to use the software.

Vindigo is a directory of restaurants, entertainment venues and stores in major U.S. cities. You download it to your Palm and carry it with you. Tell it where you're standing (in the illustration above, you're on the corner of Amsterdam and Broadway in New York City), and it will show you whatever sort of restaurant or fun you're looking for. Sorted by distance from where you are. With ratings. For free.

What a killer app! I need to tell *everyone*. This is why they invented handheld computers! *It's so cool!*

But, while that alone is grounds for this to become an ideavirus, as described it doesn't seem particularly smooth. After all, after a sneezer tells you about this cool software, you've got to remember the name (vindaloo? indigo?), go home, type it into your browser, download it, synchronize it, etc. A disaster. No way it's going to work.

Which is where the smooth part comes in. You see, right on the bottom, underneath the buttons for eating, shopping and entertainment, is a button that says "give."

So, when a sneezer is going on and on and on about how cool this is, you just take out your Palm, they take out their Palm, press the give button and sixty seconds later *the entire product is now on your Palm!*

That's smooth. It's about as close to perfect smoothness as you can get.

It goes beyond smooth. It's persistent. The next time you synchronize your Palm with your PC, it will automatically upload all the ratings you've put into the computer and get you an updated version. Instantly. Automatically.

The ideavirus has stuck.

Is it working? Well, the folks at Vindigo seeded just 100 sneezers with the original version of the program. Then they spent virtually nothing on advertising and waited to see if the virus would spread. It's now the fastest-growing application on the Palm.

Note that this isn't viral marketing in the sense that Hotmail is. You can happily use Vindigo for months without mentioning its existence to a friend. Vindigo works really well, but it also happens to be optimized for spreading the ideavirus.

Saving The World With An Ideavirus

The Prius is a new car from Toyota. And it's the only car that's ever won an award from the Sierra Club. This is the car that's supposed to save us from ourselves, to take a whack out of the greenhouse effect and to conserve our remaining fossil fuels.

How? By using an engine that's a hybrid of gasoline and electricity. By getting more than 90 miles to the gallon, giving very good performance and emitting close to zero pollution. I dearly hope it succeeds. *This car is important!*

Unfortunately, because Toyota is a factory-based company that uses ideas (instead of being an idea company that owns factories) they've built the product completely backwards. I'm confident that someday everybody is going to be driving a car as positive for the world as the Prius, but it won't be because of the way *this* car is marketed.

Let's start with the name. How can you tell someone about a car you're excited about if you don't know how to pronounce it? Is it pry-us, or is it pree-us? I don't want to feel stupid, so I just won't say the name.

Second, is there a smooth way for me to spread the word? A visit to the Toyota website doesn't even show the Prius on the home page, and when I search for it, I get a very nice page. But where's the "tell a friend" button? How can I set up a test drive? Is there a place for me to give my email address so I can give permission to get information on when the car is going to be available in my neighborhood? Alas, no on all three counts.

What about a community activism component with teenagers going door to door with petitions, hoping to lobby the local government to buy Prius police cars? Or letter-writing campaigns that spring up from grassroots environmental organizations around the country . . . ?

But the biggest mistake Toyota made was the way they designed the car. Unlike the VW Beetle and the Mazda Miata, the Prius is not a driving billboard for itself. Here's what it looks like:

You could have 1,000 of these cars drive by and you'd never, ever notice it. You wouldn't notice the styling, you wouldn't notice the gas mileage or the lack of emissions—and you certainly wouldn't aspire to own one just by looking at it.

Is Toyota on a mission from God? Are they acting like zealots, aggressively pushing a car that will change the world for the better, the most powerful idea to come out of the car industry since Henry Ford perfected the assembly line? We need *passion* from our manufacturers.

What a lost opportunity! An idea merchant in search of a virus would take a very different tack. Instead of trying to make it cheap and boring, they'd realize that the first people to buy a car like this are people with money to risk on an unproven technology. Realize that the opinion leaders and nerds who are most susceptible to this idea are also the most likely to want to drive an exceptional car.

I'd redesign the thing to be stunning. Different. Unique. Maybe a permanent bumper sticker announcing my current gas mileage on an LCD readout. Or a fleet of far-out colors. The first 50,000 people who buy this car will be doing it to make a statement. And every person who does will be making that statement to the 1,000 or 10,000 people who see them driving it. A virus waiting to happen.

Remember what I said about the VW Beetle? 180° difference.

Toyota forgot to pick a vector for this car. They don't know exactly who they want to buy it, so they designed it for everyone. Precisely the opposite strategy of the new VW Bug. But remember, an ideavirus adores a vacuum, and there is a very big and very empty vacuum just sitting here, waiting to be plucked. Toyota could have picked any vector they wanted, leading to any hive they chose, and yet they chose none.

And finally, I wouldn't let just anyone buy the first models off the line. I'd select the very best sneezers, the loudmouths, the pillars in their community and do whatever it took to get these folks to drive a car. James Bond? Julia Roberts in her next film? The mayor of Carmel, California or the head of Greenpeace?

This is urgent. This isn't about making another few million bucks from a website. It's about infecting the population with a good virus, and doing it before the vacuum fills up with junk and it's too noisy to communicate about it.

Is *Unleashing The Ideavirus* An Ideavirus?

Here is the step by step plan I'm using to turn this manifesto into an ideavirus:

1. Describe something important and cool and neat and useful and new, and do it in compelling, clear and exciting words.
2. Launch the virus to the largest audience of sneezers I can find. In this case, that means the readership of *Fast Company*. Do it with graphic splash and panache and impact.
3. Make it smooth. Post the entire manifesto at www.ideavirus.com. Include commentary from big-name authors, pundits and industry professionals. Include the entire text of not just the manifesto but the entire book. Make it easy

to send the book to a friend. Include an audio version of the book. Include my powerpoint slides. All for free.

4. Run ads and promotions to create an environment in which sneezers feel comfortable spreading the manifesto to others.

5. Maintain the virus as it grows by doing speaking engagements and distributing free copies of the hard-copy version of the manifesto to appropriate sneezers.

Moving Private To Public

One of the challenges facing oldline companies as the ideavirus becomes more important is that they're used to providing private services. Your friends and acquaintances probably have no idea what brand of PC you have, whether you have gas or oil heat, how often you see the chiropractor or what your favorite kind of wine is.

Because of the private nature of these relationships, the only way to expand the market for them is for the marketer to spend more money and interrupt more people with more junk ads. *But,* if they can figure out how to make them public, if they can figure out how to launch an ideavirus, the whole equation changes. Here's an example: your frequent flyer miles.

American Airlines has made a fortune using frequent flyer miles to induce loyalty, and just as important, to establish a currency that they sell to other companies.

But none of your friends really knows your frequent flyer habits. You almost never talk about them unless something exceptional happens that you want to brag about . . . like buying tickets for the whole family to fly to France with your miles.

There are a number of things that American Airlines can do to move miles out of the closet and turn them into an ideavirus. For instance, they could allow people to buy, sell or trade their miles. Would this lead to more mileage redemptions (a bad thing)? Sure. But it would also turn miles back into a nationwide fascination.

Far more clever would be to make the following announcement at a convention jammed with business travelers: "If you can find someone at this convention who has precisely the same number of miles as you do, we'll give you both a million miles." Suddenly, every person you meet wants to talk to you about your mileage status.

Hakuhodo, one of the largest ad agencies in Japan, used a similar approach and turned it into a national craze. It seems that sending New Year's cards is a big deal in Japan . . . much bigger than Christmas cards.

Most people buy their cards at the post office—envelope and stamp included. When you send a card, it comes with a lottery ticket, good for a small prize if the recipient wins (a bicycle, a radio, etc.).

Hakuhodo runs their promotion on the Net. And the cards are free to send (no stamps, no fee). But the best part is that if the person you're writing to wins, *you win the same prize*. So, the more you send, the happier your friends are, and of course, the happier you are.

Not only did this promotion go viral, it turned into an epidemic. In 1998, 25% of the people with Net access in

Japan either sent or received one of Hakuhodo's cards. And Hakuhodo cashed in by selling ads in each and every one of those cards.

In order to turn these public ideaviruses into useful, long-term assets, the companies that create them need to gain permission from people to follow up directly. Then, they go back to private marketing, at a very low cost, with excellent results, until they're ready to go public again with another virus.

Of course, going public doesn't mean you have to run a selfishly oriented promotion. When I was in college, the gay and lesbian center ran a campus-wide activity called "Wear jeans on Wednesday if you're gay." Suddenly, something that had been a private topic was now the topic of discussion among everyone. If you weren't wearing jeans, was that because you were afraid that people thought you were gay? Is there something wrong with being seen as gay, whether you were or not?

One simple act turned the notion of sexual preference into an ideavirus and generated thousands of hours of intense discussions about how society (and how we) viewed the issue.

You're In The Fashion Business!

Without question, the most difficult part of unleashing a manifesto is creating something that's virusworthy. And one of the key components of that art is understanding the fashion moment.

Why do clogs come and go? Bell-bottoms? Miniskirts?

How is it that every year, multiple clothing designers launch very similar clothes, without consulting with each other in advance?

Why is it that we rarely see people dressed like the two women above? Did these folks wake up one morning and go out and buy the entire outfit at once, or did it happen gradually?

Why do some Internet businesses (group scheduling, free email, health portals) seem to appear simultaneously, even though it took them months or years to launch?

The fashion moment occurs when a respected hive member takes a chance and tries out something new.

One of two things occurs when a hive member shows up with a new "outfit":

1. The hive embraces the new. They start wearing a nose ring or get a tattoo or switch from using a Filofax to using a Palm. When this occurs, the respected member gets *more* respect, becomes more influential and reinforces his position as a powerful sneezer.
2. The hive rejects the new. Many times, the person who introduces the new item will be ignored or ridiculed (this happens more to the less-respected members of the hive, but it happens to everyone sooner or later). When this happens, the person who tried to introduce the new fashion loses respect, becomes less influential and is usually less likely to try again in the near future.

Obviously, respected members are hesitant to lose their positions of influence, hence the consistency and uniformity among hives.

Some hives are incredibly conservative (go to the Association of American Actuaries annual meeting and you won't see an awful lot of surprising new innovation), while others are known for their daring (the trends introduced on the New York City nightclub scene oscillate like the NASDAQ).

Some people—I call them fashion editors—seem to have an innate sense for knowing when a hive is ready to adopt a new virus. Successful venture capitalists, journalists, chefs, research and development labs and record label executives are great fashion editors.

Clive Davis at Arista Records was a stellar fashion editor in the music business for generations. He launched dozens of breakthrough acts . . . from Aretha Franklin to Whitney Houston, Carlos Santana to Patti Smith. The only thing they had in common was that they were just right for their time. A month earlier or a month later and they might never have succeeded. (Well, maybe Aretha would have succeeded no matter what . . .)

But no fashion editor is infallible, and if they're not careful, they fall into one of two traps:

They lose touch with the hive and fall in love with their own taste.

Without the feedback loop the hive provides, they "lose their touch." Someone who had a seemingly hot hand starts failing.

Warren Buffett is a brilliant stock market investor with an extraordinary ability to understand what other people are going to want to invest in. But when Internet mania started to hit the stock market, Buffett lost his ability to predict what the hive would predict. I think he *did* know, but overruled his sense of what would happen with his own common sense. Buffett left billions of dollars of profit on the table because he refused to believe that the Internet stock ideavirus would spread across the hive of investors.

They stop thinking of themselves as fashion editors and start to believe that they are fashion makers.

Rather than acting like someone who has a sense as to what virus will hit the hive next, they believe that they are respected enough by the hive to *force* them to accept the next virus.

Fashion designers are famous for this, as are rock groups, authors and product marketers. Take a look at New Coke—the biggest flaw in the introduction of this product was that Coke believed that if they willed the consumer to adopt a new formula, the consumer would do as they were told. Instead of spreading like a virus from a respected hive member, they tried to ram the formula for New Coke on the hive of Coke drinkers. The hive rejected it.

The challenge your business faces is finding or training a fashion editor. Launching products too early is just as bad as launching them too late—if you miss the timing, you fail to fill the vacuum with your virus. Miss the timing and the profit belongs to someone with better timing and better fashion sense than you.

To those dedicated to the idea that your business is a factory, all this must sound like heresy. After all, if you wanted to go into the fashion business, you'd have gone into the fashion business! But, like it or not, we're all in the fashion business.

A few years ago, there was plenty of cherry wood to go around. People weren't making much furniture out of it . . . it wasn't in style. Then a furniture designer named Thomas Moser decided that his fashion sense was telling him that cherry wood would make a comeback. That once people saw how beautiful the wood was, the idea of furnishing your house in this warm, comfortable wood would spread through his chosen hive.

Moser built an entire company around cherry wood furniture, and bought thousands of acres of prime cherry in anticipation of demand. Today, Thomas Moser has grown more than 30% a year for the last ten years, with showrooms in New York and overseas selling $5,000 tables and $3,000 chairs. Not because the furniture is great (which it is) but because he created a fashion that resonated with his hive, because he launched an ideavirus.

The Money Paradox

The sooner you ask for money, the less you'll make.

The single biggest mistake idea merchants make is that they ask for money too soon. On one hand, you want to charge early and often, so you don't waste time on people who are just looking, and so you can maximize your income before your idea fades. "Take the money and run" is a cliché for a reason.

But this strategy introduces friction into the system. Many marketers require people to pay the most when they know the least. For example, why don't movie studios run a day of free sneak previews to get the virus started, and then charge more once everyone wants to see the movie? Today, if you want to taste a new movie, you've got to pay $8 for the hit-or-miss privilege.

On the Internet, dozens of new businesses have discovered how important this model is. A company called eFax offers a service that lets you get faxes delivered to your email box. They launched it as a totally free service. Why? Because it's scary enough to be one of the first people to try something as flaky as eliminating your fax machine. And it's even scarier to pay money for the privilege.

So eFax has a plan: get people hooked on a free system. Build an ideavirus. Then upgrade people to a paid system that offers all sorts of extras.

1. Fill the vacuum
2. Achieve lock-in
3. Extract revenue

They can fill the vacuum by getting in first and furious and spreading the virus. They can achieve lock-in by making it hard for people to switch to a competitor (what a hassle to keep changing your fax number!). And finally, they can extract revenue by offering value-added services or selling advertising.

In that order!

Will eFax be guaranteed an easy upgrade path to paying customers? I have no idea. Some businesses (like email) will be stuck at *free* forever, thus making the whole journey hard to justify. In this case, they could offer free faxes with an eight-hour delay before you get them, but for $5 a month, you get the faxes instantly. So it's free for me to try out, free to spread, but profitable after lock-in is achieved.

The challenge, of course, is to figure out which businesses have a payoff at the end. The challenge is also to be patient enough to wait, to introduce the friction of charging at just the right moment.

Watts Wacker catapulted his career by writing *The 500 Year Delta*. After this book about the future came out, people started to hand it around, to embrace his ideas. This led to larger audiences and a dramatic increase in bookings for speaking engagements. In a few months, I'm confident he made more in speaking fees than he had from royalties on the book. By letting the ideavirus grow before trying to extract much profit, he was able to make more money in the end.

In very transparent markets like the Internet, the fear is that all ideaviruses will be so competitive that you'll never be able to extract money. That's why the race to fill the vacuum is so intense. If you can fill the vacuum aggressively and permanently, it is easier to extract money.

Think Like A Music Executive (Sometimes)

There are plenty of lessons you can learn about viruses from folks in the music industry (current behavior notwithstanding, but more on that later).

First, industry executives realize that nobody buys a CD because they like the quality of the polycarbonate disc. If you don't like the idea of the music, you're not going to buy it.

Second, they realize that making money later is way more important than making money now. They learned this the hard way. Consider radio for a second. Before radio, music sales were tiny. Why would you buy a song for your Victrola if you'd never heard it before? How could you know if it was any good?

At first, radio might seem like a threat to the recorded music industry. After all, they play the *entire* song, not just a few notes. And if it's a hit song, you can hear it night and day on the radio every few minutes if you're so inclined.

For a while, the music business fought the idea of radio stations playing songs for little or no compensation. Then, in the 1950s, they realized how valuable airplay was—so valuable that a congressional inquiry discovered that music labels were bribing disk jockeys to play their records.

Fast forward a few decades to MTV. Once again, the music labels balked at supporting MTV's insistence that they provide expensively produced music videos—for free! It took a year or two for them to discover that MTV *made* hits—that giving away the music for free turned out to be the best way to sell the music.

Music execs know that you'll pay nothing to hear a song on the radio, but if you like it, you'll gladly pay $15 for the CD. And that if you love the CD, you're more likely to pay $40 for tickets to the local concert, where you might be converted to a raving sneezer, much more likely to infect your friends and neighbors with raves about the band, the song, even the souvenirs!

For some reason, history is repeating itself. Rather than embracing Napster, the software that lets millions of people listen to each other's CD collections, music moguls, fronted by the hard rock band Metallica, are once again complaining about the free distribution model.

Even if the record companies are able to beat Napster in court (a likely outcome) it won't matter. There are already dozens of technologies (like Gnutella) waiting to take its place, and each will be harder to stamp out than the one before.

Patience! Instead of hassling Napster, they ought to figure out how to license Napster and the others, probably in exchange for intensive promotion of their hottest acts. Why not let me subscribe to my favorite bands, paying for live performances or attending private concerts or buying T-shirts. I'm certain that if the Grateful Dead were still around, their primary income source would not be from CDs, but from souvenirs, followed closely by live concerts. Is that what the record companies want? Doesn't matter. It's what the network is going to deliver, regardless of how they feel.

Is the CD going to disappear? Absolutely, regardless of what happens to Napster. What will determine the future of the record business is whether music execs are able to redefine their jobs around what happens after they ignite a virus over Napster or its successor.

Is That Your Final Answer?

When a sneezer is ready to spread your ideavirus, *what should he say?*

It sounds like a simple, almost silly question, but it goes to the core of how smooth you can make your virus. If you give sneezers easy-to-follow, effective instructions, they're likely to follow them, because, after all, their goal is to spread the virus.

On "Who Wants to Be a Millionaire?" the producers insist that Regis Philbin repeat the catchphrase, "Is that your final answer?" almost to distraction. But now it's become a powerful, smooth tool for sneezers who want to spread the virus. I must have heard the phrase fifty times and read it in dozens of newspaper columns before I saw the show for the first time.

By giving loyal watchers a five-word catchphrase, the producers created (intentionally or not) a powerful shorthand for referencing the show. Hotmail did the same thing with the sig file in the free email each person sent. Right there at the bottom of each email, with no additional work on the part of the sneezer, were specific instructions on how to get Hotmail.

Buffalo Springfield and the Beatles did the same thing with some of their songs. It took just a few notes—an investment by the listener of seconds, not minutes—for them to expose their "idea" to a new listener. By working so hard on the first chords of the song, pop music producers (and Beethoven for that matter) made their products far smoother. It's easier to share the song when you can hum the riff.

For most ideas, the web can be a powerful tool to help with this. What might a website for sneezers look like?

The first touch, the first impression and first visit, must go beautifully. It's got to be fast. It should contain exactly what you've tested and discovered that most effectively captures the attention of the first time-visitor. You're in control in this moment, and you can make it work or not.

The site should also be filled with tools that make it really easy for a visitor to become a sneezer. Get out of the way. Give the sneezer something to share. Do like Tom Peters (at www.tompeters.com) and include *all* your Powerpoint slides. Don't require registration or permission at this stage. Let them in, sell them on the idea, then give them the (free) tools to share.

A Dozen Ideaviruses Worth Thinking About

Company	Big idea	How you spread the virus (the medium)
Polaroid	Instant photography	"HEY! Look at this," you say at the party.
Tupperware	The best food storage devices	Get your friends to sell their friends—multi-level marketing
Fax machine	Documents delivered by phone	The more you sell to your business associates, the better your machine works.
Home Shopping Network	Shopping via cable TV	"Hey Madge! Look what's on Home Shopping," you say to your friends on the phone.
Fast Company	Journal of the new economy	Company of Friends—monthly meetings of local fans of the magazine.
Carmine's Restaurant	Tons of food, tons of garlic	Six-person minimum for reservations—you need to sell your friends to get in.
Beanie Babies	Collectible teddy bears	If other people start collecting, your collection increases in value.
Gamesville	Super sticky games on the web	Word of mouse—email your friends and invite them over.
Hotmail	Free email	Totally viral . . . every mail you send promotes it.
Tommy Hilfiger	Urban preppy chic	Logo virus—the more you wear the logo, the more people see it.

Company	Big idea	How you spread the virus (the medium)
"The Cathedral and the Bazaar"	Open source programming works	Enabling powerful web sneezers to spread the word by giving them a powerful manifesto they can share.
Vindigo	Zagats on my Palm	"Give it to me," and a friend can beam it over in seconds.

Why I Love Bestseller Lists

One of the critical moments in the spread of an ideavirus is the question the consumer asks before diving in: "Is it worth my time/money?"

Of course, your recommendation is important to me. Of course, I want to look as good as you, be as smart as you, have as much fun as you. But I also care desperately about everyone else's opinion. After all, none of us is as smart as all of us!

The most common way this popularity is reinforced is that the user will hear about a new ideavirus from more than one person. Usually, we hear about something first from a promiscuous sneezer, someone who has some sort of benefit from making the recommendation, or at the least, someone who's *always* recommending stuff. We all know somebody who eats out every night or listens to every CD or is into whatever bizarre conspiracy theory has gripped insomniacs this week.

But then, sometimes we hear about the same ideavirus from someone else. And then another person. Finally, we realize that something is really going on, and we investigate.

In the real world, these reinforcements are usually caused by sightings or physical interactions. Riding through the New York subway last year, I encountered a kid wearing what appeared to be a black stocking on his head. But along the hem were the words, "Tommy Hilfiger." It seemed like an odd affectation and I let it go.

A week later, I saw four more Hilfiger skull caps. In the week after that, a dozen. If I were in search of genuine urban chic, I certainly would have bought one at that point, if only to protect my trademark bald pate from the winter chill.

The same thing happened with the VW Beetle. First there was one in my neighborhood (a yellow one) and then a few, and then a dozen. With all these reinforcements, I assumed that it was now a safe thing to consider, and went to the dealer to have a look for myself.

Online, the rules are very different. There is no physical world to bump into. Instead (and even better for the statistician in each of us), there are actual digital counters and accurate, up to the minute bestseller lists. No guessing. No inferences. The real scoop.

Amazon.com has a bestseller list more than a million titles long. Visit any title and you can see where it stands compared to every single other title in the world. Wow. Now we instantly understand what's hot and what's not.

MP3.com has done the same thing with music. As a track gets played more and more often, it moves up their digital bestseller list. And yes, Zipf's law works here too—the top-most tunes are downloaded far often more than those just below them.

We use the same math when we look at the MediaMetrix list of the most visited websites, or Variety's tally of the weekly box office numbers (some people saw "Titanic" just because it seemed that everyone else was). Various organizations also track bestselling cars, bestselling vodka and highest-paid executives.

One of the best ways to facilitate adoption of your idea-virus is to find a bestseller list that makes sense and then dominate it. If that's impossible, figure out how to create your own bestseller list and popularize that!

This isn't just conjecture. A breakthrough paper by Stanford Business School professor Kirk Hanson demonstrated this in a really profound way. His team artificially boosted the bestseller status of files for download on the web (they downloaded one file over and over again, increasing the counter of how often it had been downloaded). The result? Heavily downloaded files get downloaded more often! Nothing was changed but the counter, but users were more interested in seeing the most popular files. Simple, but true.

Want to launch a new drink using your company's chichi liqueur? Why not identify the right bar, frequented by powerful sneezers in the hive you're targeting. Then pay the bar to post a "bestselling drinks list." Now, bribe enough folks to go in and buy themselves a drink. Soon, you'll see your drink climbing the bestselling drinks list, and this alone ought to be enough to get other—less easily bribed drinkers—to give it a try.

Of course, sampling doesn't always lead to the spreading of a virus, but without sampling, you've got no chance, do you?

How A Parody Of *Star Wars* Outsold *Star Wars*

According to USA Today, a parody called *George Lucas In Love* is currently outselling the new *Star Wars* movie on video on Amazon. How is this possible? How can mighty Twentieth Century Fox be beat by a nine-minute, $8 handmade film?

Because the parody is an ideavirus. And because the medium of the Net is the perfect place for the word to spread.

In the old days, if you made a movie, you needed movie theaters across the country to show it. That's way outside the reach of an entrepreneur, regardless of how clever his movie is.

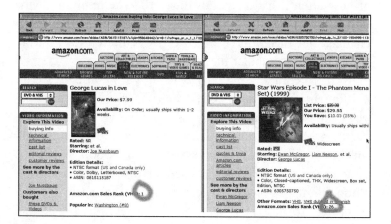

Videotape leveled the playing field a bit (Blockbuster can carry hundreds or thousands of titles), but it's still very difficult, time-consuming and expensive to force your way into nationwide distribution.

But Amazon is a different story. Amazon prides itself on carrying just about everything. Since they don't have to carry much inventory, Amazon doesn't take much of a risk by listing a title. And the entrepreneur can certainly find his tape listed along with the thousands of others available.

So distribution is the easy part. But how to spread the idea?

Well, the parody fills a vacuum. In this case, the vacuum was "funny and interesting news about *Star Wars.*" Certainly, the launch of the videotape was a yawner, the mania about the film version having largely subsided. Would many people buy the video for their libraries? No doubt. But it wasn't *news.*

But now, here's an email telling me that someone has seen the funniest little video. It's hysterical, my friend says. So I click on over to Amazon (using his affiliate link, I notice—he may be a powerful sneezer, but he's also making a profit on this virus). There, I note more than 100 reviews, all of them positive. I see that it's a bestseller. I realize that there's almost no risk here, certainly worth ten bucks and a few minutes of my time. I buy it.

And after I see it, I'll tell five friends. This time using *my* affiliate relationship.

A classic ideavirus. Yes, it would have grown faster if the filmmaker had just put the video online for free, but he was stuck in the mindset of making money now. Yes, the charge and the wait for shipping definitely slowed the virus down, but at the same time, it was a nice balancing act—a slightly slower virus in exchange for tens of thousands of dollars (and probably a contract for a real movie from a studio).

If it were me, I probably would have posted a low-resolution excerpt of some of the funny parts online . . . it's going to happen anyway, so the filmmaker might as well do it and thus control what the sneezers say while also increasing the velocity of the virus.

Wassup?

I first heard about the Superfriends parody in an email. Apparently, some clever animator had taken the soundtrack of the ubiquitous Budweiser commercial and replaced the video portion with Batman, Superman and Aquaman hamming it up and having a few brews.

Clicking on a link (pretty smooth transition from interest to exposure, you'll notice), I see that it's on a reputable site and happens to be one of the most downloaded files (a bestseller list!).

Soon, I'm laughing out loud. It really is funny. Of course, I've got to tell three friends, so I do. It's going viral.

A few weeks later, a site launches another Wassup parody. This one uses the AP photo of Elian Gonzales as the star. But this time, the virus grows far faster, with more than 100,000 people seeing it in less than 24 hours.

Why did it grow so fast? Because everyone who had seen Superfriends and liked it didn't need much coaxing to get infected by this one. By tapping into a virus-friendly base, it took much less effort for the marketer to get the message to spread.

(Of course, this is a paradox, because the ideavirus loves a vacuum. In this case there wasn't a vacuum—the Wassup parody was an old joke. So, in order to make an impact, it had to be fresh and at least as funny. But once it cleared that hurdle, the rest was taken for granted.)

This time, though, the ending of the cycle was very different. The Associated Press fired off a letter to the site behind the virus, claiming copyright infringement and not interested at all in the idea of parody and its protection. So the short movie came down.

Inevitably, if you create a piece of digital media that becomes popular, someone is going to parody it, or at the very least, use it in a way that you're not delighted with. If your digital media becomes *that* popular, odds are you should embrace it, not fight it. Budweiser, for example, has wisely let the parody virus spread unfettered. Being parodied online is a shortcut to burning the Budweiser brand further into our subconscious.

Judging A Book By Its Cover

No question, a great cover can make or break your book. Kurt Andersen wrote one of the funniest books I've ever read (*Turn of the Century*) but, by all accounts, it didn't meet sales expectations. Why? One reason is the cover, which is one of the worst I've ever seen in my life.

Remember, the search for Medusa is usually a hopeless quest. But just as it's difficult to sell someone on your ideavirus with just an image, it's also nearly impossible to suck them further in if the image is offputting, inconsistent or boring.

Boring is probably the worst offense. Whether your product is a book, a trading card, a car or even the tag on a bag of tea, boring is the obvious, but wrong, solution.

You've worked very hard on the stuff "inside." You've refined, tested, edited and slaved to make sure that the idea is powerful indeed. And then it comes time to make the package—the cover. The prevailing wisdom is to create a cover that's attractive but not offensive. Something that will attract attention from everyone and offend no one.

This is nonsense, of course. It can't possibly attract everyone and offend no one. The very best cover images are like a cold glass of water thrown in your face. They break one or more rules of graphic design or industry rules of thumb. They play off existing images but change them in a vital and important way. They're loud. They attract the eye, but they also hold it. And most of all, they intrigue us enough that we need to understand what's inside: we set ourselves up to be exposed to the virus.

When Yahoo! first launched, the company name and logo broke every rule in the book. But co-founder Jerry Yang will be the first to tell you that in a world populated with Lycos, AltaVista, InfoSeek and Architext/Excite, Yahoo! was the easy winner. Easy to spell. Easy to type. Easy to tell other people about.

And it had personality. It meant something.

Was it risky? I don't think so. A boring, hard to spell, meaningless name like Lycos was risky.

Being The Most

Turns out there's been a battle going on for a few years—the battle to make the hottest hot sauce in the world.

At the beginning, you made a hot sauce by using peppers. Hotter peppers made hotter sauce. And a sauce made from Scotch Bonnet Peppers (the hottest peppers on Earth) was the hottest sauce on Earth.

Then, some nutty scientist figured out how to extract just the essence of hotness from Scotch Bonnet Pepper puree. By using gas chromotagraphy or some other evil technology, he was able to create a sauce more than 1,000,000 times spicier than your basic pepper.

Why does this matter? Because being the hottest hot sauce ever made is like being the Mona Lisa. Because if I've managed to eat chili with the hottest hot sauce ever made in it, I'm going to tell my friends. I'm going to spread your hot-sauce virus. If it's the second or third hottest, who cares?

There's always room in any list for the world record holder. The greatest basketball player who ever lived, or the nastiest restaurant owner, or the fastest computer. It's noteworthy. It's news. It's worth sharing.

My dad's hospital crib company dominates the market, making most of the cribs that are used in hospitals around the world. Their standard models cost $700 to $2,000 each, and they last forever. How to grow the business? How to get more attention and more sales?

His engineers found a leading hospital, and together they designed the best (and the most expensive) hospital crib in the world. With all the options, it costs about $7,000. Yet it's selling like crazy, from the Philippines to Tucson. Why? Because it's worth talking about. Because it embodies an idea, and it's an idea worth sharing.

Google.com has plenty of traffic, yet they've never spent a nickel on advertising. How? Because it's the fastest and most complete search engine ever built. Electronically amplified voices—from nerds to magazines—are happy to trumpet the idea that there is a faster, better way to search than using the tried and true favorites.

As you think about a corporate virus or a personal one, consider: What you are the *best* or the *most* at? How can you refine and amplify those traits to create a Wow! product . . . a world's record holder that is worth mentioning?

And by the way, if you're not facing a vacuum (and most of us aren't lucky enough to be in that position) you've got to be ten times better than what's already there, if you're going to start your own virus.

In Defense Of World Domination

Targeting isn't enough. Being a world record holder isn't enough either. You also need to dominate your hive.

Having 5,000 loyal, rabid fans of your ideavirus is great. Unless, of course, your audience is the population of Massachusetts. To dominate Massachusetts you need a lot more fans than that. Without the power of reinforcement, your virus will peter out. Unless individuals are hearing from sneezers again and again, your virus will slow and will probably die out over time.

Imagine, instead, that you have 5,000 fans at Stanford University, which is a hive with a population of about 15,000. The chances that you'll be exposed to every other member of the hive are huge. Why? Because if each one of the 5,000 fans tells just a few other people, you're already hitting each person more than once. And if the idea is virusworthy, that's probably enough to dominate the entire campus. Even the laggards will surrender when they see everyone else is doing it (even the accounting department at my old company did the Macarena at the company Christmas party).

Malcolm Gladwell calls this the tipping point—the idea that creating and propagating an ideavirus is not enough. The biggest win comes the last time your virus doubles in size. The biggest win comes when you've so dominated the hive that the last folks (who are often the most profitable folks) can't help but come along. They tip because they hear from so many respected sneezers that they feel they have no choice but to get on the bandwagon.

This happened with AOL. A few years ago, AOL was paying $300 in marketing costs to get one new member. All those CDs that showed up in every magazine were expensive, but they were effective.

But how could AOL justify spending $300 to get a member who had a lifetime value of just $124? Jan Brandt, the genius behind the campaign, realized that if she could win at this expensive part of the curve, the game would soon turn in her favor. She knew that once she got over the hump and dominated the hive of people about to go online, the next generation of users would come along far cheaper.

She was right. Once AOL established dominance for new users, they established a network of powerful sneezers. Powerful, because these were folks who until quite recently had been new users. These once-new, once-lost users had the credibility to spread the word to those just behind them on the learning curve. They were powerful because they'd been there, and their personal experience counted for more than any salesperson's could.

The virus had authority, because every "bestseller" list credited AOL with being far and away the most popular Internet service provider in the land. Today, someone at Sun City who until recently had no idea what they were talking about when they said "Internet" could proudly recommend AOL to the person in the next condo. AOL now spends about $100 in marketing to get a new member—because their virus tipped.

There's plenty of interesting action that occurs before the tipping point, though. Viruses need to spread before they tip, and a smart marketer can be quite happy indeed along the way.

Dominating the hive is essential in starting the virus in the first place. And most marketers make the mistake of picking too big a hive to focus on in the first place.

If you go to the Consumer Electronics Show in Las Vegas, you'll see one of the largest trade shows in the world, and you'll also see hundreds of companies spending millions of dollars trying to dominate the show. All of them fail. Which is why it's so rare for a virus to be launched at the CES. It's just too noisy, and there are no exciting but safe recommendations for the most powerful sneezers to make.

The smart marketers take a different path. They launch at Demo or Spotlight or Esther Dyson's conference—a much smaller venue, but a higher concentration of powerful sneezers. Here, for about the same money as making a whisper at CES, you can completely dominate the discussion.

If You're A Member Of The Academy, You Go To Movies For Free.

If there's an association of powerful sneezers, it's the Academy of Motion Picture Arts and Sciences. This association of actors, screenwriters and directors has celebrated movies every year for nearly a century, and every year it seems to get more popular and more influential.

If your movie wins an Oscar, you can count on a blip at the box office, and even better, a long, profitable life on video. And of course, any actor who wins one has a label that will enhance his career forever.

So, how much do the studios charge Academy members to go to a movie? That's right, nothing. Not only that, but the studios are delighted to deliver the latest movies to an Academy member's home, on her choice of VHS or DVD.

Why? Why give the movie away? Well, here it should be pretty obvious. The leverage that comes from building buzz among Academy members more than pays for the cost of sharing the movie with them. In fact, the benefits are so obvious that studios like Miramax have been accused of trying to buy the Oscars by throwing hundreds of thousands of dollars of trade advertising at Academy members.

Well, if this is so obvious, why bring it up? Because your idea, regardless of marketplace, has a similar group. Maybe it's not as easy to find or as easy to reach, but there are powerful sneezers in the audience for almost every idea. It's the money paradox, but on a much smaller scale. Finding these sneezers and giving them a sample of your idea for free is a no-brainer. Even better, figure out what it costs to deliver it with impact.

I met with a marketing executive from Hong Kong recently. He's building a company that is targeting the health care and financial services industries. He's got a big idea, and if he can persuade some of the key sneezers in the industry, then most of the other companies are sure to follow.

The good news is that he was invited to speak at a gathering of 100 top chief information officers from the financial services industry he's targeting. The bad news is that he was planning just to give a speech.

What an opportunity! What a chance to talk to all the key sneezers at once and dominate the hive. We did the math, and it's clear that even if he needs to buy each one of the attendees a BMW to get their attention, it's worth it.

When you have an opportunity to dominate not just a hive, but the sneezers *in* the hive, you need to spare no expense to do so. Don't just give a speech about how your product works well. Fly in three satisfied customers to tell their stories in person. Don't just give a speech and ask for questions. Sponsor a cocktail party afterward so you can meet individuals and answer their questions. Don't just give a speech about how your product is safe and secure. Give each attendee a first aid kit for their car. By focusing on this key moment, by over-investing, you can lay the foundation for a virus to come later.

How An Ideavirus Can Drive The Stock Market

When you think about it, the stock market is nothing but thousands of ideaviruses. (That's right, thousands. An ideavirus doesn't have to dominate our entire culture to be an ideavirus . . . some last for just a few days in a very isolated hive, then disappear.) When you buy a share of stock, you don't really get anything—just the right to sell that stock to someone else tomorrow. So if a positive virus catches on and the demand for the stock skyrockets, you win.

The market's respect for ideavirus thinking starts before the company even goes public. Choosing an investment bank for your IPO is a first step. Firms like Goldman Sachs and Alex Brown are powerful sneezers (even though they can easily be bought off with millions of dollars in investment banking fees by eager companies looking to go public). If one of these firms aggressively recommends the stock to institutions, the virus starts off on the right foot. The alternative—marketing the stock through a smaller, less respected (and perhaps cheaper) investment bank—is almost certain to lead to a lower return.

The next step is pricing the IPO. The current rage is to underprice the stock being offered to the public, because that will lead to a huge first day appreciation in the stock. It's not unusual for an IPO (like Globe.com, Martha Stewart Omnimedia or Street.com) to dramatically increase in price on the first day of trading.

Why do this? Why leave all those proceeds on the table so that the folks lucky enough to buy into your IPO make the money instead of your company? The answer is simple, and it has two parts:

First, by rewarding the powerful sneezers who are lucky enough to buy into your IPO, you maximize the chance that they'll participate and will tell their less powerful (but more numerous friends) about this exciting new investment.

Second, the rapid rise in the first day of trading allows other powerful sneezers (the news media and brokers you don't have direct contact with) to talk with excitement and amazement to the next group of potential investors. In other words, this is cheap marketing. It's a way of communicating news (this is a hot stock) to large numbers of people in a powerful way.

After the stock is public, the company has its work cut out for it. There's a multi-layered community of intermediaries between the stock and the people who want to buy it, and the company must work the hive to find the most powerful sneezers able to spread the word about the stock.

The first stop is the market analysts who cover the stock. Once again, the marketplace sees this group as being powerful sneezers (when one analyst recommended Amazon.com, the price of the stock doubled in just a few days). By courting the analyst community, a company can find a way to communicate the story they've created around the stock.

Don't underestimate the power of the story. There are almost no other cues available to persuade someone to spread the word about a stock. You can't see it or touch it or smell it—it's just an intangible right to make money in the future. As a result, the story must be able to describe the reason why the stock is selling for x today but will be selling for 3x tomorrow.

Brokers are a fascinating component in the spreading of an ideavirus around a stock. Remember, they're not paid unless people trade. Buy and hold is the enemy of most stockbroker compensation schemes, since they only charge for trades and are paid by commission. Yet, for many decades, brokers were seen as powerful sneezers, especially if they helped make you money in the past. In fact, they've always been promiscuous sneezers, motivated (whether in the short term or the long term) by their ultimate financial gain. A "good" broker is one who realizes that if he postpones financial gain in exchange for helping his clients make money in the long run he'll get more and more clients.

All this is changing as the world shifts to trading online, and more important, getting stock news online. Suddenly, anyone can talk about stocks, anyone can post to a bulletin board, and anyone can spread a rumor.

As a result, stock ideaviruses spread much more often and much faster. In one case, the public markets knew about a CEO's plan to quit before his board of directors did. Because the individuals who post these notes are anonymous and possess unknown motivations, the chances that they'll develop into powerful sneezers is slight. But the sheer number of posts (more than 100,000 a day on Yahoo!'s bulletin boards alone) means that they have influence.

An astute CFO or CEO can look at the key factors in the creation and spread of a stock ideavirus and launch a campaign to move the virus with a velocity and vector they're comfortable with, and more important, aim it at the appropriate hive.

Note, for example, that some stocks, like Iomega, are the darlings of online stock bulletin boards. As a direct result, those stocks are far more volatile than the average. Live by the sword . . .

Yahoo! has worked hard for years to manage the story about its stock. Gary Valenzuela, the legendary former CFO at Yahoo!, was obsessed with three things:

1. Become a blue-chip stock, one that institutions would happily own.
2. Become profitable, to distinguish the Yahoo! story from its competitors.
3. Underpromise and overdeliver, always beating the "whisper numbers" that analyst established for the company's quarterly earnings.

As a result, Yahoo! stock has consistently and regularly outperformed its competitors. And due to the success in labeling Yahoo! an Internet blue chip, the stock is much less susceptible to swings due to rumors.

Was that expensive in the short run? No doubt. When the market was looking for good news and hype, Yahoo! often refused to deliver. Short term gains were forsaken for building a story, a story that could become an ideavirus to be delivered by analysts and other powerful sneezers.

One way to predict the future of a stock, then, is to see beyond the story and understand whether the company is actively managing the ideavirus, and doing it in a way that will move it to the right hive.

Bumper Sticker Marketing

Years ago, I was a walking parody of a high-tech yuppie.

I worked as a poorly compensated marketer at a start-up software company in Cambridge, Massachusetts. I drove a dented old Saab. I used a Macintosh. And on the back of my Saab I proudly affixed a bumper sticker that read, "I'd rather be driving a Macintosh."

This is an ancient form of ideavirus marketing, of course. I used my car as an amplifier, exposing my message to hundreds or thousands of people. But even better, given the neighborhood I was driving in, I was focusing the message on an appropriate hive, and given the car I was driving, adding power to my sneezing.

Think about it. If the bumper sticker had been on the back of a junker Chevy, rusting outside an abandoned farm in Oklahoma, you would have had a very different response to the message, no?

The neatest thing about this technique is the way Apple converted the private (what sort of computer do I use) to the public (my proclamation of how happy I was to be a Mac user).

There are countless opportunities for marketers to do precisely the same thing today. And not just on your bumper. Some marketers ride along with their product—the Ralph Lauren pony, for example, is advertising on the front of your shirt all day long. Others manage to make it a more political choice—Marlboro, for example, was one of the ten largest marketers of imprinted clothing a few years ago.

Picking the medium for your "bumper sticker" is important, but it's just as important to determine *why* someone is going to be willing to stick his neck out to promote *your* product.

Personal pride is an excellent tactic! If people are willing to sneeze on your behalf because they're proud of you, your product and their association with it, you're in. Now all you've got to do is give them a smooth way to spread the word.

No, You Go First!

The challenge of the new idea is that very few people want to go first. Who was the first to swim in the Charles River in Cambridge, Massachusetts after years of it being off limits for health reasons? Who was the first to give their kid the chicken pox vaccine? Which company chose to be the first to file its taxes electronically?

One of the key reasons to launch an ideavirus is that you can give people a risk-free, cost-free way to check out the safety of your idea *before* they commit. And more important, you can create an aura around your idea—an aura of inevitability, of invincibility. When everyone is buzzing about a new technique, tactic, service, musical style, club, food—whatever—it's easier to put fear aside and try it.

But just as people are hesitant to be the first to buy a fancy new product, many are hesitant to try a fancy new idea. There are plenty of people who want nothing to do with a new song or a new book . . . they're happy to wait until it's been screened, filtered and accepted by the mainstream.

So, depending on the hive you choose, you need to make it clear to that consumer that your idea has *arrived.* That the water's warm, the air is safe to breathe and your idea is a comfortable, tried and true one.

One way to do this is with bestseller lists. And with testimonials. And by exposing the digital word of mouth record to let them see the countless people who have tried it and liked it. Do it with the specific objective of reminding people that others have taken the risk and happily survived. If you work at this and do it on purpose, you'll be amazed at how much water you can drain from the river—how easy it is to bring the rocks to the surface, how powerful you can make the message when you expose the connections that led you from person A to person B. It's in this sort of active ideavirus marketing that many brands are able to run rings around the competition.

Even before you do this, offering your idea in trial-sized, bite-sized portions is critical. Many companies have created neat, effective online products, only to see them fail because they required consumers to go through a time-consuming download before they could use them. If consumers can't use it, they can't understand why they want it! Catch-22: a product you don't know if you want to download until you download it.

Of course, if you can't try it first, you can't decide if you want it. Give them a version instead that doesn't require a download and doesn't work as well—but still makes their life better. Why? Because now that I've sampled it without risking taking a lot of time to try to understand the arcane intricacies of downloading in Windows, *now* I'm willing to invest the time to do it.

Digital Media Wants to Be Free

When was the last time you bought some table salt?

Odds are, you didn't pay very much. Salt is cheap. Why? Because once you own a salt mine and pay for a salt factory, the cost of making a pound of salt is low indeed. But because there's more than one salt mine out there, the competition for getting salt sales is pretty intense. And given that all salt is pretty much the same, why pay more?

Pricing battles are certainly not unusual in physical goods. In fact, almost every competitive category of item that's entirely physical (without an idea attached) uses cost-based pricing. In other words, it's a commodity. When those rules are abandoned (as they were with crude oil during the Arab oil embargo) consumers are shocked and angry.

For a number of reasons, this pricing approach hasn't really kicked in with intellectual property. It only costs McKinsey a few hundred bucks to write a report for Chrysler, but they happily charge a few million dollars for it. One more copy of a Bob Dylan CD only costs 80 cents to make (less than a vinyl record!) but it sells for twenty times that.

Why?

The biggest reason is that intellectual property is rarely a commodity. There are many kinds of salt, but there's only one Bob Dylan. And when you want to listen to Dylan, it's not clear that 10,000 Maniacs is an acceptable substitute.

Because intellectual property is unique, it has long resisted a trend toward commodity pricing at the margin. In fact, the price of most forms of intellectual property has *increased.* Barring one big exception: Stuff that went from being expensive to being free.

The most popular web server software (the programs they use to run most giant websites) is not sold by Microsoft. And it doesn't cost $10,000. It's free.

The most popular web browsers are free. The cost of listening to a Beethoven concerto went from $30 (at some fancy theater in London) to $0 after radio was invented. The cost of watching a movie on network television is zero. The mathematics of the ideavirus make it too compelling for the creators of viruses to stay greedy.

The more people know your virus, the more it is worth!

Thus, if charging people for exposure to your virus is going to slow down its spread, *give it away.*

Apple just cut the price of WebObjects software from $50,000 a copy to $699. That's a 98.7% decrease in the price.

Why? Because Apple realized that unless a lot of people use their software, no one will use it.

Take a look at www.mp3.com. Pick an obscure music category like Celtic. Go to the end of the bestseller list: there are 1,168 songs listed. These are not illegal copyright scams, where the music has been stolen from the artist. These are real songs, posted by the artists or their labels. The whole song . . . not part of it.

Why would anyone do this? Give away an entire album of music when Bob Dylan can charge $16?

Look at it from your point of view. An unknown artist *is* a commodity. An unknown artist *is* the same as a box of salt. If you don't know why the artist is unique, why pay?

Look at it from the artist's point of view. The cost of giving away songs is literally zero. Once an artist has made a record, the cost of one more copy of an MP3 is nothing. And if it helps him get listened to, if it helps him build a virus, then he's one step closer to no longer being a commodity!

In fact, many artists would *pay* people to listen to their MP3 cuts if they thought it would help them break through the clutter and get famous. Take a look at the Payola section of MP3.com. You can do exactly that—pay money to have your song promoted so you can give it away for free.

Of course, once you're famous, you can go ahead and charge $16 for your CDs.

Or can you?

Sure, there's going to be room for collectibles. For live events. For autographed guitars. But once something is no longer hot and fresh and the latest, rarest thing, why wouldn't the self-interested artist go ahead and give it away free to stoke the ideavirus for the next release? In a competitive marketplace where there's transparent information about who's listening to what, the Internet becomes radio. And artists know that charging radio stations is dumb.

This same logic applies to books. And to just about any other sort of digital media you can think of. Unless there's a unique property of the media being offered, I maintain that sooner or later it's going to be free. The Bloomberg, a machine used by stock brokers, for example, commanded a huge price premium for years, because the combination of excellent data and locked-in user interface meant it wasn't worth switching. But as the web replicates more and more of the data available, it's inevitable Bloomberg's market share will decrease—and their prices will as well.

The exciting thing is that people who go first, who put their previously expensive digital media out there for free, will gain the lion's share of attention and launch bigger and longer lasting viruses.

So. Who wants to go first? And who wants to go . . . last?

Van Gogh Lost His Ear To Prove A Point

When Vincent was painting, he often sold his work for just enough money to cover the cost of paints and canvas. Back then, his ideas and his paintings were one and the same, and neither was held in very high regard.

Over the last hundred years or so, something has changed. Instead of selling for $200, or $2,000 or even $20,000, it's not unusual to read of a $10,000,000 sale of a Van Gogh. Over time his paintings have increased in value with each sale. But the paintings haven't changed at all, have they?

What's changed is the value of his ideas and the popularity of his ideas—not the ideas themselves. It's easy to get a reproduction of a Van Gogh. For a few hundred dollars, you can even get a painted reproduction that only a trained expert can tell isn't the original. So why pay twenty million dollars?

Because you're buying a souvenir. An expensive souvenir, no doubt, but a souvenir nonetheless. The original painting is a priceless keepsake that reminds you of the idea Vincent Van Gogh first unleashed on the world. And unfortunately for Van Gogh and his heirs, it took far too long for the ideavirus to spread.

Compare this inexorable and dramatic increase in value with the resale value of a newspaper.

Today's newspaper is "worth" fifty cents to a dollar. The combination of recent news and events in one handy packet makes it a reasonable purchase. However, yesterday's paper is virtually worthless. And if you've got a big stack of them, you're going to have to *pay* me to take them away.

Why? What happened? Simple: the newspaper is a vessel for ideas with very short half-lives, and once the ideas aren't fresh any more, they're worthless. Imagine, though, how much you could sell *tomorrow's* paper for—especially if you sold it while the stock market was still open.

This is a lesson in one way to make your digital media valuable: keep it fresh. It's getting harder and harder to do; they used to send Charles Dickens' serialized novels over here by boat—news that was three weeks old was considered fresh—but that doesn't mean you can't succeed.

By focusing on souvenirs and speed, creators of digital media can create two effective ways to profit when we play by the coming new set of rules.

But How Would We Make Money?

So how is a bookstore to make money? Or a publisher? Or an art dealer or a consultant or a music label?

The biggest objection to ideavirus thinking is that it represents a substantial change from standard operating procedures. Successful companies are in no hurry to rock the boat . . . especially if it represents a significant change in the status quo and a risk to planned-for revenue and profits.

Mightywords (an Internet publisher) is aggressively targeting traditional book publishers and re-sellers by creating a new online business that cuts out all the middlemen and lets authors sell works (preferably 15 to 60 pages) directly to readers. Go to their site and you can find thousands of these mid-length pieces, priced from $3 to $30 each.

Mightywords gets half the revenue, the author gets half, the reader gets insight and wisdom and everybody wins. By creating new markets for mid-length ideas, the company seems to be filling a niche. Of course, then they can turn their success into dominance by integrating up the food chain until they disrupt all the competition in the publishing world and profit mightily.

So you'd think that the concept of ideaviruses would be attractive to this maverick company. After all, they're only a few months old.

Not true. It bugs them terribly to give away ideas, because it flies in the face of their brand new business model. After all, if an author profits most by giving away her work, how does Mightywords make money?

If you catch yourself asking this question about a new business model innovation ("How would we make money?") you're headed for trouble. The Internet doesn't care how you make money. The Internet isn't going to wait while you figure out how to react. Instead, there's some crazy entrepreneur who's willing to spend years of his life making you miserable by wrecking your business model.

Email didn't ask the fax companies if it was okay with them if a new, instant, permanent, digital communications tool came along and wrecked the fax business. Match-maker.com didn't hold meetings with the extremely profitable video dating services out there to find out if it was okay for them to launch. Who cares if Matchmaker.com never makes money? What matters to the existing businesses is that these new kids on the block have wrecked the business landscape for the old providers.

Giving digital media away is a reality. Non-dominant players in any industry will always succeed more by giving away digital content and then profiting later than they will by holding back to preserve somebody else's business model.

It was a mistake for the record companies to fight radio and MTV. It's a mistake for them to fight Napster. Rather than fighting to patch the leaky bucket, perhaps they could redefine their roles so they can figure out how to profit from a "free" world.

Crossing The Chasm With An Ideavirus

In his brilliant book, *Crossing the Chasm,* Geoffrey Moore unleashed a powerful ideavirus about how new businesses and new ideas get spread. Basically, there's a chasm in the product adoption cycle.

The curve used to look like this:

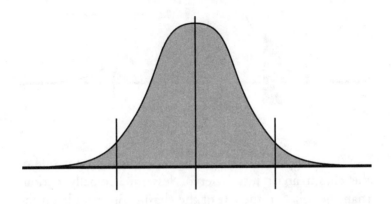

On the left are early adopters, the nerds who love new stuff, who want to get their hands on anything neat and potentially wonderful. On the right are the laggards, who are still having trouble getting rid of their steam engine cars.

The meat is obviously in the center. That's where the vast majority of us live, and where the combination of big audience and pretty decent pricing is most attractive to a marketer.

In the old days, people believed that you could introduce a product to the early adopters, use the high profits from those sales to ramp up production and advertising, and then roll the product out to the masses.

There's a problem with this view: there's a gap in the curve. A chasm.

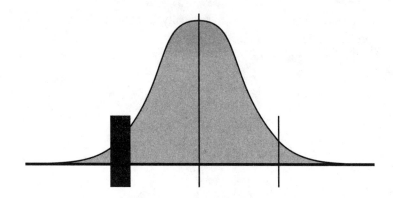

What happened? Turns out people on the right side of the chasm aren't just lazier or less intellectually curious than the folks on the left of the chasm. But people on the right are *fundamentally different* from the folks on the left. How?

Pre-chasm people want something cool. Post-chasm people want something that works.

A nerd wants the latest personal digital assistant. An executive wants to keep her appointments straight.

A cutting-edge IT guy at Allstate wants a device that will use satellite technology to update claims instantly. The CEO at Nationwide wants something that will reduce costs.

A fashionista wants the latest haute couture outfit from Paris, regardless of how ridiculous it looks. The party girl wants something that'll get her a hot date next week.

The foodie wants maple-jalapeño corncakes, layered with crème fraiche and bourbon. The hungry person just wants something to eat.

As you can see, focusing on the folks who will give you early feedback and be your initial sneezers, your first customers, and probably your start-up's employees is a one-way ticket to doom. Their advice will help you make stuff that's expensive, heavy, hard to use, awkward and difficult to understand. You'll be the darling of some well-respected sneezers, and then you'll fail. This is why many ideaviruses start with plenty of powerful sneezers but end up dying.

It happened to Apple with the Newton. It happened to Microsoft with almost every product they've ever launched (Bill Gates is to the far, far left of the chasm—that's why it takes Microsoft to version three to build something that catches on). It happened to Reebok and to Stephen Sondheim and to Lou Reed. In every case, they indulged the pre-chasm audience and lost the big wins on the right. (Of course, in some cases—like Microsoft—sheer staying power is able to *force* you over the chasm.)

The challenge in launching an ideavirus is to understand who the pre-chasm sneezers are, and using them but not letting them use you. In other words, they're the ones who are most likely to embrace your new idea and talk about it, but if you don't get past them to the rest of the curve, you're doomed.

Why do Woody Allen movies consistently sell so few tickets? They're certainly adored by critics, nominated for awards and attended by a core group of sneezers. The reason is simple: the virus hits a chasm. There's a huge gap between the Woody Allen audience and the rest of the population. Because of this chasm, the word rarely spreads as far and as wide as a broader message could.

The success of his latest movie, "Small Time Crooks," points to the problem. This movie has box-office results that rank among the top four he's ever released for one simple reason. During the month it was released, it was the only decent family movie available. By focusing (intentionally or not) on creating a wry, funny movie that was understandable at many levels and worth bringing your kids to, Woody crossed the chasm. Suddenly, the sneezers were saying, "This is a great movie for your family," instead of saying, "This is another great Woody Allen movie."

Some viruses are just never going to cross the chasm. Try as they might, the computer nerds are having no luck at all getting normal people to start using Linux. And the guys who sell the hottest hot sauce in the world are just not going to find their product on the table at TGI Friday's restaurant.

But that's okay. It's okay because these idea merchants understand that the hive they're targeting is *not* everyone. They understand that if they choose the right hive, it's okay if it's small, it's okay if it's not everyone. The caveat, of course, is to match your expenses and your expectations to the size of the hive you've chosen. If you spend big on product development and marketing, figuring that will get you over the chasm, it better.

The Myth Of The Tipping Point

One of the most seductive ideas in Gladwell's *The Tipping Point* is that somehow a magic moment appears when the entire population goes from blissful unawareness of your offering to total and complete infatuation.

While this certainly appears to happen, it's not a reality for most companies and most ideas, and it's not even a requisite for mindblowing success. There are two related reasons for this.

The first is that it ignores the power of the hive. The chances that you're going to launch an ideavirus that consumes the entire population is slim indeed. After all, there are seven billion people out there, and all of them have very different needs and communication cycles. Even if you just boil it down to the United States, or to Republicans with Internet access, it's pretty clear that large hives very rarely tip about anything.

The second reason is that winning and tipping aren't the same thing. In order to really win with an ideavirus, you have to concentrate your message very tightly on a specific hive. But even then it's not clear to me that you have to tip to win.

Let's take a look at eBay for example. By almost any measure, eBay is a winner. It's employees are millionaires and billionaires. Early investors are delighted. Users are happy, with time spent on the service going up all the time.

But has eBay tipped? Certainly not in terms of awareness among the general population. When asked to name an online service, only a tiny fraction of the population picks eBay as their first choice. But it gets even more obvious when you ask people where they go to buy and sell used junk. The vast majority of people are still using classified ads and garage sales, *not* eBay.

Yes, the management of eBay is on the cover of *Fortune* and *Business Week* at least once a month, or so it seems. Yes, every meeting at certain high-tech companies includes the sentence, "But will this allow us to become the eBay of [insert business here]." Within a very small, very focused, very profitable hive, eBay *is* a winner. But it didn't happen because some magical tipping process took place. It happened because a smart, focused, powerful ideavirus started and spread across a concentrated hive of investors and pundits, and this led a tiny company to have a huge stock market valuation.

The reason I point out this myth is that it's dangerous. Dangerous because it leads idea merchants to believe that if they just wait long enough, something will happen and make them tip—like Yahoo! or the Atkins diet or Nike or the Macarena. I don't buy it. The odds are with you if you focus on small hives filled with pre-chasm sneezers, and then obsess with crossing the chasm as fast as you possibly can. If you tip, that's a bonus.

The Compounding Effect

One of the factors that makes the tipping point myth seem more real is the power that comes from multiple sneezers. While one or two recommendations might make for a smooth transition, there's no doubt that as the number of powerful sneezers recommending an idea to you increases, the chances that you're going to use it *dramatically* increases.

This is a genuine side effect of the tipping point. As you are surrounded by hive members who loudly sneeze about a new idea, the greater your chances of at least trying the idea. Rather than decreasing returns, as we find in advertising, there are actually increasing returns from an ideavirus. The more people who have it, the more you want it.

Are there iconoclasts who fight every trend? Of course. They wouldn't be seen in a hip car or a hip restaurant or listening to a pop tune. But for most individuals, in most hives, the compounding effect is quite strong.

Thus, one of the most essential tasks an idea merchant can accomplish is to bring all positive news to the forefront. He then makes every hive member *think* that every other hive member is already converted to the virus, thus creating the self-fulfilling prophecy that leads to success.

Publishing houses do this when they print lots and lots of copies of a book and ship it out to stores. If there are tons stacked up by the cash register, many people think that this must be the hot new book, so they buy it. On the basis of this trial, the book shows up on the bestseller lists soon after being published. This, of course, leads to more people trying it, because, after all, it's on the bestseller list. So, without any genuine "word of mouth," the book has established a much larger foundation. It won't get any bigger unless the idea is virusworthy, but at least the book got a shot.

On Eric Raymond's webpage promoting his essay "The Cathedral and the Bazaar," he lists and points to critiques of his work. Why? Because bringing these critiques (both positive and negative) to the forefront is an excellent way to bring the compounding effect into play.

Most marketers focus on getting organic word of mouth going without taking the time to lay a framework for the compounding effect. Music Direct, on the other hand, goes to great lengths to leverage powerful sneezers. On their site (www.amusicdirect.com) they list the recommended recordings of several high-end stereo magazines. Each one is linked directly to their online ordering service. Thus, you can read a review in *Stereophile* and know that you're only a click away from buying it on their site. Look at a few of the lists and you'll notice that the same record shows up more than once. Boom. Even if you weren't considering buying that title, the fact that three trusted sneezers have recommended it makes it much more likely that you'll consider it.

The folks at Telarc Records learned this lesson early on. Unable to compete with the big boys at the other classical music labels, they recorded the Cincinnati Orchestra playing dramatic renditions of songs that only a stereo lover could love. Big cymbals. Cannons. You get the idea.

Then, they worked hard to get high-end stereo shops to use the CDs they were recording to demonstrate their equipment. Thousands of consumers who might never have rushed out to buy another recording of Tchaikovsky's "1812 Overture" now discovered that Telarc's recording was being used anytime they listened to $5,000 speakers or $3,000 amplifiers. Hey, if you were willing to drop 20 large on a stereo system, certainly it was worth a few more bucks to have the best CDs to play on it, wasn't it?

Bill Gates' Biggest Nightmare

One of the repeated mantras during the Microsoft anti-trust sideshow was that middleware threatened the very essence of Microsoft's cash cow: the Windows OS.

Basically, middleware is software that sits on top of the operating system on your computer and talks to the Internet or other programs. Once you develop a killer piece of middleware, it doesn't matter what operating system you're running—the middleware works the same. The first successful example of middleware was the browser, but you can be sure there will be more.

I recently spoke to a woman named Louise Wannier who developed a piece of software called enfish. You can find it at www.enfish.com.

What if there were a piece of middleware that was designed for people who had an "always on" connection to the Net. And what if that software let you automatically track your stocks, your email, your calendar, your instant messages—all the stuff you spend time doing online, but in an organized way, and all at once?

If you're like me, that accounts for the vast majority of time you use the computer. Suddenly, Windows is obsolete.

Sounds like it's time for Louise to start shopping for a new Porsche, no?

But there are some problems. And all of them are related to the idea she's created and how to turn it into an ideavirus.

Problem #1: In order to use enfish, you have to download code. Experience has shown us that this is a huge amount of friction with which to saddle a new idea. Basically, you can't enjoy the software until you go through the pain and suffering of downloading and installing it.

Products like Shockwave and various forms of software that must be downloaded (like wallets) have shown us that it can cost as much as $100 in direct-to-consumer marketing expenditures to get someone to download a piece of software. In the case of enfish, this is way, way too much.

Solution: Get rid of the download if possible. If not, make it swift and painless.

Problem #2: This is a private experience. Unlike ICQ or Hotmail, which are both based on communications and are thus pretty viral, enfish saves you time by organizing *your* life and *your* data, and so you're not naturally inclined to spread the idea. In other words, it doesn't do its own sneezing, nor does it reward you for sneezing on its behalf.

Solution: Make it public. Let people post their bookmarks and layouts for their co-workers. Figure out how to turn it into a communications tool because communications tools are the most likely to go viral.

Problem #3: It's not very smooth. It's awfully difficult to describe what enfish does, because it's not simple. Its biggest strength—that it solves a problem you didn't know you had—is also a huge hassle when it comes to marketing the thing. "Free Email" is smooth indeed. "Automated organizer for always-on Internet knowledge workers that saves you three hours a day" is not.

Solution: This is the hardest one. Breakthroughs frequently have this problem. Figure out how to teach the sneezers what to say . . . even if it means giving them a pre-written email to forward to friends.

Problem #4: There's no existing amplifier. There are plenty of sites where people talk about cars or hobbies or restaurants. Find a hive and you can talk to them. There are magazines about gardening and starting Internet companies. There are TV shows about cooking and the weather. But there's no natural way to amplify a message about the problem that enfish solves. There are few easily identifiable hives that are just sitting there, waiting to hear from enfish.

Solution: Use advertising to feature your most satisfied users.

Problem #5: The ideavirus isn't a natural monopoly. In other words, once they do a great job of spreading the virus, it's not clear that enfish's solution will be the only one to triumph. One of the amazing things about ICQ, for example, is that the better they did, the better they did. In other words, there were network effects that created a natural monopoly. Unfortunately for enfish, there isn't an obvious reason why an enfish knock-off couldn't be as good as enfish.

Solution: The same communication tools that made it go viral will also support its position as a monopoly.

The good news is that once it catches on, enfish will be extraordinarily persistent. It will sit on your desk for years, saving you time and making enfish a profit as they go.

The other good news is that because the benefit delivered by enfish is so awesome, once the virus starts to spread through a hive, it ought to spread with high velocity, and with the support of the very best kind of powerful sneezers. This is a product that can easily attract the attention of sneezers on the left side of the chasm (the early adopters) but also offers very real benefits that will make it fairly smooth to transfer to the right side of the chasm.

So what should enfish do?

My recommendation is that they focus on a single hive: people who trade stocks online.

Why?

Well, the hive is pretty easy to talk to. There are eight or so online brokerage companies who could all benefit by sneezing about enfish to their best customers. And online traders talk to each other constantly, meaning that the message can spread through this community with enormous velocity.

Further, the benefit to online traders is easiest to describe, so it's a lot smoother: Make more money by trading in a more organized way.

There's also a vacuum here. Nobody else is offering this value proposition to this audience.

And finally, because online traders tend to be more technically astute, the friction induced by the download will be less of a barrier.

After infecting the trader hive, will the enfish virus jump to other hives? Perhaps. But in order to do that, enfish needs to make two significant changes to their product (remember, the best ideaviruses are integrated right into the product, not tacked on at the end by the marketing department).

The first change is to create significant benefits to users that derive from enfish's scale. In other words, create a network effect so there's a natural monopoly.

The second change is to create clear and obvious incentives for existing enfish users to evangelize and bring in new enfish users. These could be simple bribes, but it's more effective if the incentives are related to the product—making it work better when you have more buddies involved.

If they can accomplish these two tricky tasks (so tricky you'll notice I haven't even told you how to do it!), then the odds of the virus jumping from the trader hive to the Net audience at large increases dramatically.

Hey, Skinny!

One of the most successful books of the last five years has been *The Atkins Diet*. Dr. Atkins has sold more than seven million copies of his books . . . with almost no advertising.

How does a marketing phenomenon like this happen? Conventional marketing wisdom says that he would need to spend tens or even hundreds of millions of dollars to motivate the one out of every 40 Americans who has rushed out and bought his book.

The secret to the book's success is that the diet was virusworthy. Unlike other diets, it really generates remarkable results in a very short time (let's leave the health discussion for another book).

But being virusworthy isn't enough. It was also smooth. All you had do to tell someone what diet you were on was say one word, "Atkins." Because the author became synonymous with the diet, it was easy to spread.

But the real secret was amplification. Word of mouth could never generate seven million conversions, not without being amplified.

So what was the amplifier? Your skinniness! Whenever the diet worked, nosy and proud friends would ask the dieter, "Hey, skinny! You look great. How'd you do it?" And the dieter would proudly respond: "Atkins."

This self-fueling virus saved Atkins millions. And it would never work for transcendental meditation, St. Johns

Wort or reflexology. Nobody is going to notice your inner peace, after all. Yes, we may be obsessed with the way we look, but it also leads to powerful viruses.

If you doubt the power of this, take a look at all the tattooed kids on the beach.

Get Big Fast? The Mistake So Many Companies Make.

Why was there so much bloodletting among consumer e-tailers this spring? How did Boo.com burn through more than a hundred million dollars in start-up cash? Why is Salon.com, arguably one of the most literate sites on the web, floundering?

The answer for almost all these high profile sites is the same: Get Big Fast isn't always the right advice.

Remember, an ideavirus adores a vacuum. So many companies, especially those racing to be the first to fill a vacuum, spend a huge percentage of their funds trying to prime an ideavirus by buying huge amounts of poorly executed, poor performing interruption advertising.

Big-spending interruption marketers hope the following:

1. That sheer bulk will make this bad advertising work.
2. That sheer bulk will scare off the competition.
3. That an ideavirus will be spawned and they will become instantly and permanently popular.
4. That once they are a center of an ideavirus, their truly flawed business model will magically make sense. Sort of the AOL effect—you can't be profitable if you're small and illogical, but if you're big and illogical, you can make

a fortune from the companies that pay you because you have the attention of a huge market.

They also fear:

1. That someone else will come along and spend more and move faster than they do.
2. That if they take their time, the market will realize that their business model is totally flawed and they won't be able to get any more funding.

Alas, the pursuit of an ideavirus has confused their analysis. Instead of viewing themselves as a natural monopoly, as virusworthy, as needing to fill a vacuum, they could have considered a very different analysis:

1. The ideavirus space for "online merchant" is already filled. It's filled by Amazon, and to a lesser, more twisted degree, by eBay and Priceline.
2. Given that the big space is filled, they ought to understand that the virus they're going to spread is going to be far smaller and far more quirky. Thus, the win is smaller, but the good news is that they'll need far less money to get there.
3. Once you accept the second point, you can realize that growing a virus slowly is actually a better strategy. Why? Because you get to perfect your business model as you grow, and you get holistic, organic virus growth, instead of the forced growth a Super Bowl ad brings you. In other words, you actually get to earn the people who visit your site.

Diamond Organics (www.diamondorganics.com) is following this approach, and it's working. Instead of trying to be a category killer and spending tons of money to persuade the world that their organic-vegetable-by-Federal-Express business is a good one, they're instead focused on delighting one customer at a time.

By spending little and scaling a lot more slowly, Diamond is able to build serious sneezers, sneezers who are quite powerful and need little additional inducement to spread the word. By getting their systems into shape they avoid the pitfalls that struck ToysRUs.com last Christmas.

But doesn't this fly in the face of the ideavirus mantra? In many ways it does. It also challenges the permission marketing idea that once a consumer solves a problem, they're not in any hurry to find someone else to solve the same problem, so vendors can achieve lock-out.

The problem with implementing the grow-slow strategy is that you might not get the chance. If you're a CEO or marketing executive in a new business, you're subject to the Catch-22 of rapid business development. You can't grow (and you can't get funded) if you don't make promises, but those promises might not be able to be kept. And if the promises aren't kept (ToysRUs.com failing to ship in time for Christmas) or the promises cost too much to keep (Boo.com) it doesn't matter anyway, because you'll be bust. So most entrepreneurs make the promises anyway, even though they realize that organic growth is the better strategy.

So, there has to be a middle ground. And the middle ground that makes the most sense to me is to not launch a business that can't sustain an ideavirus. And second, not to force an ideavirus to happen before the market is ready for it.

My best example is Amazon. My firm belief is that if Jeff Bezos had launched it a year later or a year earlier, it would never have worked. A year too early and there wouldn't have been enough sneezers and the medium wouldn't have been ready to spread the word. A year too late and the market would have been so overheated that his promise would have never broken through the clutter and attracted the attention of sneezers in the first place.

It's hard for me to imagine how a $50 million marketing campaign is ever appropriate for any business to launch an ideavirus. If you need to interrupt that many people, you're doing something wrong. Sure, you need that much (actually, much more than that) to launch a brand and to do traditional marketing. But if you're virusworthy, you generally can do it for a lot less money than that.

So you need to match the speed of your virus not just with the money you raise but also with the promises you make to your investors. Yes, Hotmail and Netscape and ICQ and eBay grew fast, fast, fast. But that doesn't mean you will. Optimize for the virus and build it into your company—or expect that it isn't going to happen.

The Heart Of Viral Marketing

Remember, viral marketing is a special case of the ideavirus where the amplifier for the virus is built right into the product. And the hot spot for this wonderful self-propagating process is in communication products.

Let's take a look at the history of interpersonal business communication over the last 120 years:

Stamps
Telegraph
Telegram
Telephone
Telex
Fax
Conference Calls
Federal Express
Cell Phones
Videoconferencing
Email
The Web
ICQ and Instant Messaging

It's a pretty extraordinary list. Twenty-five years ago, when I got my first real job, we had no voice mail, no web pages, no fax machine, no cell phones, no pagers and no email. I sometimes wonder what we did all day!

So why is there such rapid innovation in this field, when, at the same time, we are still using precisely the same Qwerty keyboard found on the early typewriters and the same pink "while you were out" message pads that came with the first phone?

The answer is pretty simple: Each one of these devices creates long-term profits for its inventor but is spread at a relatively low cost. And the reason it spreads? Because of viral marketing.

Communication products demand viral marketing because they're worthless without someone at the other end. Metcalfe's law tells us that the value of a network increases with the square of the number of people using it. So when there are 10 fax machines in the world, that's 25 times better than when there were just 2.

Once I buy a communications device, two things happen. First, I become a powerful sneezer, telling all my friends to buy one so I can send them stuff. And second, provided it's a tool that uses an existing channel (like FedEx or Hotmail), every time I send someone a message, it's selling the medium.

The story of Post-It notes is so good it ought to be apocryphal but it's actually true. Nobody was buying them. 3M was going to cancel the whole program. Then the brand manager of the product persuaded the secretary of the chairman of 3M to send a case of Post-Its to the secretaries of the chairmen of the other 499 Fortune 500 companies.

Suddenly, the most powerful sneezers in the most powerful companies in the country were sending around memos, all containing comments scrawled on Post-Its. It took just a few months after that for it to become yet another successful business communication device. A classic ideavirus.

When I was in business school, a classmate spent a year working on a secret project he wouldn't tell anyone about. Turns out he was working to launch MCI Mail, the first commercial email system. It's a shame he couldn't tell anyone, because a bunch of us would have been happy to tell him what we knew, even 20 years ago: An email system isn't going to work if there isn't anyone to send email to!

MCI was charging about $100 to set you up, and another $20 or so a month, plus usage, for this new service. Big mistake! They inserted friction early in the process, ensuring that people would never try it, especially so early in the virus's life.

My idea was that they give MCI Mail, plus a computer to send it with, to 50 people in each of the top 100 companies in a given industry. *Free.* Suddenly, that industry's leaders would be communicating with each other fast and frequently. It would change the culture of the companies. The virus would spread. MCI would win.

What's the lesson? There are two:

- If you can somehow convert your idea into a virus that has to do with communication, it's much easier to make it go viral. The best sort of communication is an actual communication tool (like the fax machine or instant messaging) but inventing words, new musical concepts or other ways people communicate goes a long way as well.
- Find the powerful sneezers and beg, cajole and bribe them to use your new tool.

The Great Advertising Paradox

Imagine for a second that there was a machine your company could buy. Figure it costs anywhere from $1 million to $100 million. You're promised by the salesman that using this machine can transform your business, dramatically increase sales and profits and turn your business into a success.

Interested?

What if the salesperson also tells you that companies who don't buy the machine have a hard time growing and often languish . . . and then she points out that one company, Procter & Gamble, spent more than $2 billion on machines just like this one last year. Interested?

Oh. There's one caveat. Actually two:

The ongoing output of the machine can't be measured. You have almost no idea if it's working or not—and there's no guarantee. If it doesn't work, tough.

Still interested? Well, after those caveats, there's just one more fact to mention: On average, the machine only works for about one out of every ten companies that use it. Ninety percent of the time, the machine fails to work.

By now, you've probably figured out that I'm talking about advertising. Mass market advertising is one of the most puzzling success stories of our economy. Companies spend billions of dollars to interrupt people with ads they don't want about products they don't need. The ads rarely work. Ads that are created by less than competent ad agencies and clients almost *never* work. One day, I'd like to write a book about the worst ads ever run, but my fear is that it would be too long.

Now, writing off all marketing expenditures because most of the time they don't work isn't the right answer, either. Hence the paradox. You can't grow without it. But you often can't grow with it, either.

So if advertising is such a crap shoot, such a dangerous venture, why do it? Because for the last 100 years, the single best way to determine whether a company was going to get big or stay small was to look at its advertising. Time and time again, aggressive companies with great advertising—regardless of their industry—have managed to make the ads pay and to grow and become profitable.

So what changed?

A few things. First, the clutter in the marketplace has finally made advertising even less effective. A threshold has been crossed, and with hundreds of TV channels, thousands of magazines and literally millions of websites, there's just too much clutter to reliably interrupt people. Add to this the "consumerization" of business-to-business sales (with more ads directed at businesses than ever before) and the explosion of dot-com advertising, and it's easy to see that the game is fundamentally different.

So, what should we do about it? Consider the ironic situation that MarchFirst, Inc. finds itself in. MarchFirst was formed in 2000, the result of a merger between USWeb/CKS, which does websites and consulting and advertising, and Whittman-Hart, an Internet consulting firm.

According to the *New York Times,* MarchFirst wants to launch with a bang, so they've announced a $50,000,000 advertising campaign designed to "cut through the clutter" and to "get the name out there, to create strong brand awareness," according to Robert Bernard, their CEO.

How are they going to do this? By buying full-page ads in newspapers and Internet trade magazines, by running TV commercials during sporting events, and even running ads in lifestyle magazines.

Now, be honest. If you're flipping through a magazine or surfing through channels on TV and you come across an ad that is based on "the human desire to be first," will you stop and pay attention? Will the slogan "a new company for the new economy" make you sit up and take notice? Will you give up a few minutes of your precious time to read an ad about a company you've never heard of, which solves a problem you probably don't have? Not bloody likely.

Surely there's a better way for this company to spend $50,000,000. Surely there's a more effective way to start a relationship with the 10,000 people who matter to them than interrupting millions of us over and over and over.

Old-fashioned, hand-crafted, fun-to-make, sorta-fun-to-watch interruption advertising isn't going to disappear altogether. But it's just a matter of time before CEOs and investors start measuring their ever-increasing ad budgets with the same critical eye they use for every other insanely expensive investment they make.

Permission: The Missing Ingredient

When Hotmail launched their free email service, they did almost everything right. They built a product that was worthy of an ideavirus. They made is smooth. They built amplification right into the product. They approached the right people and started with just enough push to make the thing take off.

But then they made a huge error.

They forgot to get permission to follow up. They failed to ask their users (the folks who were infected by the virus) if it was okay to send them an anticipated, personal and relevant email every week. They didn't build an asset.

As a result, the Hotmail website has one and only one way to make money. By selling banner ads. And nobody clicks on banner ads when they're reading their email. So advertising on the Hotmail site is super cheap. And probably overpriced.

We're talking a multi-billion-dollar mistake here. If they had permission to follow up with 20 million people every single week with an email that was filled with useful information and relevant ads, they could easily sell the slots in this email for a buck a week. That's a billion dollars a year in lost revenue, which, using stock market multiples, is a gazillion dollars in market cap. All because they forgot to ask for permission.

Let's face it: It's unlikely that every single idea you come up with is virusworthy. If we're going to have to grow our businesses in a reliable, predictable way, it's unwieldy to have to depend on an ideavirus catching on every time we want to grow. We still need a way to communicate with people directly, to do it when *we* want to, to talk to the marketplace without a filter.

Advertising used to be the way to do this. But what a waste! What a waste to have to pay a magazine for an ad to reach a user you already have! You've got a pair of Nike sneakers in your closet. But Nike has to buy an ad to reach you—they don't have permission or the ability to talk to you directly.

Same is true with Stevie Wonder. You bought "Innervisions" because you heard it at a friend's house, or on the radio, not because you saw an ad. Yet when Stevie comes out with a new album, his record label has to start all over again, interrupting you using mass media. Both Stevie and his label waste a huge asset every single time you buy an album. They have no idea who you are, and worse, they don't have permission to contact you again.

The challenge of the idea merchant is to turn the virus into an asset. And you turn the virus into an asset when you ask the user for permission to follow up directly!

This is probably the biggest mistake that ideavirus marketers have made to date. They launch a virus—a website, a book, a record, a software program, a food—and enjoy the fruits of the virus while it lasts, but fail to gain a long term asset. And without that asset, they can't launch new products or leverage their existing ones without long lag times and the high costs associated with contacting the users they've already converted.

How A Virus And Permission Team Up To Find Aliens

Turns out that the best way to find alien life somewhere in the universe is to listen. Specifically, to use powerful supercomputers to scan the spectrums for anomalous sounds.

Unfortunately, there isn't a supercomputer available that's powerful enough to get the job done in our lifetime. Which is why the SETI built the largest distributed computer network in the world. More than 2,000,000 computers are working, in their spare time, to process these huge chunks of data.

The mechanics of the system are elegant. Whenever your computer has some downtime, a screensaver pops up, and behind the scenes, your Pentium processor starts cranking through data that the computer downloads through the web. But what's really neat is the fact that all 2,000,000 computers in the network signed up without any advertising or financial inducement.

Instead, the SETI project launched an ideavirus. Word spread among nerds the world over that they could help find alien intelligence by having their computers participate in the network. It's a classic ideavirus, propagated by some powerful sneezers.

The power of the network, though, comes from the fact that they don't have to relaunch the thing every week. That it's incredibly persistent, of course (once you set it up, it stays set up until you take the initiative to turn it off), but even better, they have permission to communicate to their users.

This permission is an asset. You can measure it. You can leverage it. You could turn it into cash if you wanted to.

Let's take one more look at the sequence:

1. Invent a virusworthy idea.
2. Make it smooth and persistent.
3. Incent powerful sneezers.
4. Get their permission to follow up.

The Art of Creating an Ideavirus

So far, much of what we've discussed is science. Mathematical formulas, game theory, categories of individuals. This is stuff you have to do well to allow your virus to take hold. And as the understanding of propagating viruses increases, companies will get better and better at the tactics.

The hard part, though, is building the virus in the first place. The hard part is inventing an idea that's so compelling, so Wow! that it spreads through the hive with high velocity, converting everyone in its path.

How is it that some ideas move so quickly while others just languish? Why did the Apple Newton fail so badly, while the Palm took off just a few years later?

Caveat: If I knew the answer, I'm not sure I would tell you! To date, no one has come up with a repeatable formula for creating viruses in a reliable way. There are precious few people who are serial virus starters.

My hope was that this would be a long chapter, and I could answer your big question about *how*. Alas, I don't know. I know it when I see it, but I fear the rest is art.

Which means you win by trying. And failing. Test, try, fail, measure, evolve, repeat, persist. It's old fashioned and hot and dusty and by no means guaranteed to work. Sigh.

Is He Really More Evil Than Satan Himself?

The Google.com search engine is perhaps the most effective and accurate way to search the web. Why? Because instead of reading every site and trying to understand the content of every page, Google just reads the *links* to sites, and selects the pages that plenty of other sites link to. This way, popular pages rise to the top, and it's harder to trick the engine into pointing to your page by loading up on clever phrases.

Anyway, a few months ago, if you typed, "More Evil Than Satan Himself" into the Google search engine, the top link it would return was Microsoft.com. Other links that followed involved mostly Bill Gates.

How did this happen? How was it that enough hackers, nerds and online intelligentsia building web pages had a strong enough opinion about Bill & Co. that they would go to the trouble of creating links to Microsoft that used the words like evil and Satan?

Regardless of the dynamics of the virus itself, there's no question that it's pervasive, that it will take years to erase and that it cost Microsoft dearly. By filling the vacuum and creating an ideavirus of Microsoft as an all-powerful demon, trouncing anyone who came into its path, the company's critics brought the Justice Department knocking on its door.

Intel and Cisco have similar market share in the computer space. McDonald's has similar impact in the fast food business. There are plenty of companies that could have attracted attention. But because Microsoft (through its actions—and inaction) spawned a virus, it was easier for its critics to get the attention of the government. Regardless of your position on the case, it's clear that the negative virus (and Microsoft's actions that reinforced that impression) affected the judge's ruling.

Case Study: Why Digimarc Is Going To Fail

Looking at the world through the ideavirus lens makes it easier to prognosticate about a company's success or failure. Consider the case of Digimarc.

Digimarc is a fascinating idea. Create a tiny series of dots that can easily be hidden in a magazine ad. Then, if a consumer wants to go to the advertiser's website, all they have to do is hold the magazine up to the camera connected to their PC, and Digimarc's software will read the dots and automatically take the user to the company's site.

Charge the advertisers a tiny fee per ad and everyone wins! The magazines win because it makes their publications more useful. The advertisers win because it creates a direct and impactful link between the consumer and the ad. And the user wins because she finds special promotions or discounts on the site . . . without having to type in a pesky URL.

So why is it going to be an utter failure?

Because there isn't enough money in the world to turn this into a success, and the shortcut path of creating an ideavirus isn't going to happen any time soon either. I know that I'm going out on a limb here, as this technology has just been featured in *Wired* and other magazines and has gotten a lot of press. Still, bear with me . . . .

First, there are few sneezers. The participating magazines have agreed to run full-page ads promoting the service (if it helps their advertisers, it's well worth it) but other than that, who's going to talk about it?

There are no promiscuous sneezers. No individual is compensated in any way for spreading the word. There are no powerful sneezers. It's not such a great, awe-inspiring or even totally neat thing to do with your computer. There aren't overwhelming discounts or secret bits of information, because, after all, if the advertiser was willing to give a discount to a Digimarc user, he'd probably be willing to give it to everyone, right?

In addition to having a hard time describing why the service might be virusworthy, it's not smooth, either. In order to even find out if you *like* the service, you have to buy a PC camera ($100, plus the hassle of setting it up) as well as download and install a piece of software on your PC to run the thing.

Once it is set up, it's not clear if it's persistent. The incremental benefit of each use of the service doesn't appear to go up—you don't get better and better rewards the more you use it. So, as the novelty wears off, the likelihood you'll keep using it and keep sneezing about it is small indeed.

Finally, they forgot to focus on just one hive. The ads are running in a wide variety of magazines, targeting a wide variety of users. Because there's no overwhelming concentration in just one hive, the odds of the virus popping are small indeed.

So, wise guy, what would you do instead? Well, I'd re-orient the launch from a general mass-market consumer to a very vertical business-to-business offering. For example, imagine putting it on the factory floor. Now, instead of a technician having to drop everything and type in a URL to see a certain page in a manual, he could just hold up the shop manual to the camera on his already configured PC. Once you can show that it makes an overwhelming difference in just a few shops, the word can quickly spread across the hive.

If I really wanted to find the consumer market, I'd focus only on the techiest markets (like the readers of *Wired,* but I'd create a benefit to promiscuous sneezers within that market. Rather than creating a flat environment (each ad goes straight to the user), I'd introduce an email component that rewards the few people who came in at the beginning for emailing their techno-friendly friends.

My guess is that if Digimarc values the advertising at retail, they're probably going to spend $300 for every regular user they get. In order for it to be profitable, my guess is that they need to get that number down to $3. Problem.

Why Are These Cows Laughing?

If you were in Chicago last summer or lucky enough to walk through Manhattan this June, you may have noticed a few cows in the street. Actually, hundreds of cows. Big fiberglass cows—practically life-sized—located on heavily trafficked corners.

The cows cost under $2,000 to make, yet when they're sold in a charity auction at the end of the cow invasion, they'll go for $10,000, $30,000 . . . up to $50,000 a piece.

What happened? How did a $2,000 cow turn into a $50,000 cow?

Well, it helps that the cows are painted by local artists. Some are poignant, some are whimsical, but they're all extremely interesting.

However, that doesn't explain the whole thing. After all, it's a used cow, having sat out in the rain and sleet and soot for months. Add to that the fact that the cows are well-designed, but the artists behind them are by no means famous. In fact, it's fair to say that in most cases, the price of the cow will be among the single highest price these artists have ever received at auction.

A $2,000 cow turns into a $50,000 cow because of amplification. The same cow sitting in a SOHO gallery wouldn't be famous. The same cow straight from the artist would just be art, not a souvenir of a special moment in the history of a city.

Literally hundreds of articles have been written about the cows. But more important, tens of thousands of conversations have occurred. It's impossible to walk down the street with a friend and pass a cow without mentioning it. After all, it's a *cow,* just standing there in the street.

Like all good art, these cows create conversations. But unlike art in an art gallery, these cows are amplifying the number of conversations. By sitting there. Every day. Calmly. Sort of like—cows.

As you pass more cows and different cows and provocative cows, your litany of cow lore increases. Your ability to talk in interesting ways about the cows increases. "Hey, if you think this cow is cute, wait until you hear about the cow I saw downtown. . . . "

All of which goes to say that street art, performance art, guerrilla marketing performances . . . any sort of interruption of our regular routine can lead to a moment of conversation. When Abby Hoffman and the Yippies dropped dollar bills in the middle of Wall Street during lunch hour, they generated a virus among the people who were there, which spread to the media and beyond. By getting people to interact in a way that they weren't accustomed to, the Yippies created more impact than they would have if they'd spent five times as much cash running an ad.

While this sort of interruption of routine is highly amplified, it is by nature not very persistent. If you keep interrupting the routine, the routine stops being routine and the interruptions are. If they kept the cows there for years at a time, they'd be boring. If Abby Hoffman dropped dollar bills every day, people would quickly stop being excited by it.

That's why the bar for interruption and guerrilla marketers keeps moving. You can't do what created buzz yesterday, because there's no way that's going to create more buzz today.

Never Drink Alone

Alcohol manufacturers have two spectacular advantages over most marketers. First, there's a huge profit margin built in. Second, drinking is a social phenomenon, perfect for spawning ideaviruses.

Yet, given this natural platform, most distillers are lazy and just buy a huge number of interruption marketing events—

billboards, magazine ads, liquor store displays. They work sometimes—remember, all vodka is the same, yet people gladly pay double for Absolut. Most telling of all is the fact that St. Pauli Girl and Becks Light are made on precisely the same brewery line in Hamburg, yet people will insist that they prefer one over the other.

Despite their successes, though, virtually all of the money spent on liquor advertising is wasted. Last year, alcohol marketers spent more than a billion dollars advertising their wares, but you probably can't even name the top 20 advertisers off the top of your head.

It's more effective for alcohol manufacturers to focus on advertising to your friends, not to you, to invest in building viruses that make it more likely that the group will discuss a brand and eventually order it . . . or at the very least, admire the person who does.

One of my favorite examples was reportedly created by the brilliant marketer Bob Dorf. When Dorf was a PR guy, I'm told he was hired by Galliano to turn their obscure liqueur into a nationwide phenomenon. Realizing that there wasn't enough money in the world to buy enough "Drink Galliano" billboards, he took a very different tack. He riffed on an invention by a California bartender named Harvey and decided to popularize the Harvey Wallbanger.

Harvey was a fairly primitive cartoon, a bit better drawn than Kilroy. But he was also a drink, a drink that coincidentally used a lot of Galliano.

Dorf then set out to teach the newly-counterculture 1970s drinking crowd about this fun (hey, it was a cartoon) drink. He printed T-shirts, taught bartenders how to mix the drink and even sent people into popular bars and had them order the drinks (loudly).

The result was an ideavirus. When one fashion-forward powerful sneezer in a group ordered one, he'd have to stop and explain to everyone else in the group what it was. That group took the news to the hive, and the virus spread.

The virus wasn't particularly persistent (from what I'm told, a Harvey Wallbanger wasn't that good) but it was extremely smooth. After someone told you about the drink, all you had to do to get one was say, "I'll have one too, please." High velocity, the virus did exactly what Galliano had asked for . . . it put the drink on the radar screen.

The Power Of Parody

The sequel to *Mission: Impossible* had a huge summer opening. People talked about the trailer, and more important, told their friends to go see the movie after they'd been.

But how was Warner going to encourage people to see it two or three or four times? How to get to the hive of media-friendly, time-wasting teenagers just sitting around looking for ways to spend money? Most important, how could they cost-effectively remind people that MI:2 was out there and worth seeing again?

They decided to unleash an ideavirus that parodied their own movie.

Mission: Imp is a five minute long web film designed to go viral. It features almost famous Hollywood stars, better than usual production values (for a web virus) and best of all, a "send to a friend" button.

Unfortunately, it's not very funny—so while the foundation is there, it's not as virusworthy as it might have been if it were made by someone who wasn't nervous about offending Tom Cruise. Either way, though, it's a smart and aggressive way to get out there and start a virus to keep a product in the public eye.

Bee Stings And The Measles

My friend Kate was on a canoe trip in Algonquin Park and was lucky enough to find an outhouse on a deserted island. Relishing the chance to relieve herself without having to dig a hole in the woods, she rushed in and sat down.

Bad news for Kate, there was a beehive inside. Forty stings later, she found herself sitting in the lake, waiting for the pain to subside. After a long paddle back to base camp, she got herself to a doctor. The good news is that after a little pain, she was back to normal. Unfortunately, she's now extremely sensitive to bee stings, and has to be ever vigilant, lest she develop an allergic reaction.

Compare that to the childhood ritual of getting the measles. You get the measles, you sit through a week of an annoying rash, and then you're done. You're never going to get the measles again. You're immune.

In the first case, exposure to an invading poison led the body to become sensitized. In the second, it led to immunity. Your ideavirus might behave in either way.

Yes, in general, the ideavirus adores a vacuum. It will spread faster and farther when no similar virus has preceded it. The idea that you can follow a leader to great success might work in the old economy (like Schick in razors or Burger King in fast food) but it clearly isn't a winning strategy in the new one.

Here's the interesting special case: Sometimes, after being sensitized by one ideavirus, the market is more susceptible to a new one. The failure of the Newton, for example, made early adopters and sneezers more aware of the PDA concept (a computer in your hand), and it paved the way for the Palm to succeed. The second Thai restaurant in a given town is more likely to turn a profit than the first one. Michael Jordan wasn't the first basketball hero by any means, but our desire to *have* a hero, as sparked by earlier stars like Wilt Chamberlain and Larry Bird, made it easier for Michael to walk in and fill a role that had to be filled by someone.

But Isn't It Obvious?

One of the big challenges I faced with *Permission Marketing* and now with *Unleashing the Ideavirus* is that a lot of stuff in these books seems pretty obvious. It's obvious that marketing to people who want to be marketed to is more effective than interrupting people who hate you. It's obvious that word of mouth is more powerful than ads. It's obvious that the winner takes all online. It's obvious. . . .

But precisely because it's so obvious, it needs to be written about. Defined. Measured. Because it's so obvious, it's easy to fall into a 100-year-old habit and start doing business the old-fashioned (expensive but easy) way.

After all, if ideavirus marketing is so obvious, why does eToys need to raise $100 million in venture capital to pay for old-fashioned advertising? Why are the TV networks having their best year ever in advertising revenues? Why do really smart businesses suddenly turn stupid when faced with ad opportunities like Planetfeedback.com?

Because to embrace ideavirus marketing techniques you also have to accept a change from the status quo. And many of the executives who are now in charge made their way to the top by embracing the status quo, not fighting it.

It's much easier to raise venture money with a plan that says you're going to spend $30 million or $60 million dollars on traditional advertising than it is with a plan that says you'll only spend $3 million but employ elegant but difficult techniques to get the word out.

It's much easier to run the marketing department of a Fortune 500 company around the command-and-control interruption techniques that got the company there in the first place than it is to allow the customer to be in charge. And it's more difficult to devote your research and development efforts to building ideaviruses than it is to stick with the traditional incremental improvements.

Even marketers have heroes. Some kids grow up wanting to be like Sandy Koufax or Bart Starr. But most of us imagined creating the next great TV commercial or building the next great brand. We envy the folks who built Coke or Nike or Starbucks or Star Wars. But all these heroes found their success in a different world—in a factory-based, interruption-focused marketing environment.

Today, the world is suddenly very different. Almost without exception, every single win on the consumer side of the Internet has been due to marketing, *and the most effective part of that marketing is about the ideavirus.*

Hotmail, Yahoo!, eBay, Amazon, GeoCities, Broadcast.com, Google—all of them succeeded because an ideavirus was unleashed and spread.

So, yes, the underlying tenets behind the ideavirus are obvious indeed. But executing against them, fighting the status quo, getting it right—that's not obvious at all.

Your Company's Worst Enemy

She might just work in your office. She's certainly underpaid. And not very well respected.

I'm talking about the folks who staff your customer service department. Admit it—you and most of the folks in your company would be delighted if you never heard from or about these guys and what they do. Their job is to make angry customers go away . . . quietly.

In the old days, this was a pretty easy job. After all, very few people went to all the trouble to find your mailing address, get an envelope, get a stamp and write a letter. And if you sent the writer a coupon good for a few bucks, well that was the end of the story.

Today, it's very different. Planetfeedback.com makes it easy for angry customers to find you. And they can carbon-copy their congressman or the FAA or ten friends.

With digitally augmented word of mouth, an angry customer can leave an online record . . . one that lasts for centuries! There's no statute of limitations online.

Take a look at www.deja.com/products/at_a_glance /glance.xp?PCID=11819&PDID=32765. As I write this, more than 90 people have ranked a certain DSL provider as one of the worst providers of DSL service in the country. Actual comments:

Don't make this mistake

This is a Mickey Mouse operation. Actually, that's an insult to Mickey Mouse. Their tech support is incompetent, their customer service is a front, and their technicians are useless.

Impossible to get a live person through customer service. Sent over 7 emails and have gotten back one reply. Had to cancel because of this and they charged me an additional $150 for early termination. Completely bad attitude.

- Once the consumer has volunteered his attention, get permission.

  The goal of the ideavirus marketer is to use the virus to get attention, then to build a more reliable, permanent chain of communication so that further enhancements and new viruses can be launched faster and more effectively, under your control this time.

- Amaze your audience so that they will reinforce the virus and keep it growing.

  Where are the Cabbage Patch Kids? Why do some viruses burn out more quickly than others? The simplest reason is that marketers get greedy and forget that a short-term virus is not the end of the process, it's the beginning. By nurturing the attention you receive, you can build a self reinforcing virus that lasts and lasts and benefits all involved.

- Admit that few viruses last forever. Embrace the lifecycle of the virus.

  Cats was a terrific success on Broadway. But even great shows don't last forever. By understanding that the needs of the virus change over time (and that the benefits received change as well) the marketer can match expenditures to the highly leveraged moments.

The Future Of The Ideavirus: What Happens When Everyone Does It?

Interruption marketing (the kind they do on TV) is doomed to fail, because each marketer who enters the field has more to gain by adding to the clutter than they do by trying to make the medium work for everyone else. It's the classic

Fraudulent Thieves

Took my $100 deposit (in October!), didn't deliver a thing, and won't give it back (they deny having any record of it). Their "customer care" people use a wide variety of lies to string you along. STAY AWAY FROM THESE PREDATORS!!!

Now, this provider may be running a first-rate organization. But there's no way to tell that from these comments. Question: How many expensive full-page ads will the marketing department have to run to undo the damage that these public posts are going to do to their brand for years to come?

Compare those reviews to these for Worldspy.com:

Pound for pound the best . . .

After trying AltaVista, I had about given up on the notion of a "useable" free ISP. I then stumbled upon WorldSpy . . . I've never gotten a busy signal through WorldSpy and consistently connect at 52kbps or higher. I've never been disconnected and love the lack of an ad banner blocking my view.

Great so far

Thanks to all for your reviews that helped me find this service. I imagine it is tempting to keep something like this a secret in order to keep good service for those in the know. I know I considered that before I wrote this review! But I felt that as I benefited from others' recommendations, I owed it to the Deja community to share my experiences. I have now been using WorldSpy for a few weeks, and have been pleased with it.

Now, we're not comparing apples to apples here (Worldspy is free) but that only reinforces the point. The 290 or more people who posted positive reviews are busy telling all their friends about this service, spreading the positive news. (NB that Worldspy just tanked. An ideavirus does you no good if you can't stay in business.)

Finally, take a look at the reviews for Big Planet. They have more than 1,000 reviews, but it turns out that many of them are posted by Big Planet affiliates, looking to profit from bringing on new users.

Thus, we see one ISP on the road to failure because it appears that they've refused to invest any time, money or training in the way they treat customers. We see one that has used a very different business model (free) and combined it with excellent quality and customer service, and we see a third that's busy paying promiscuous sneezers to spread the word. *What's your company doing?*

Instead of putting your weakest people into customer service, what would happen if you put your best there? Instead of asking for reports on how much pain they're alleviating, why not let them tell you about how much joy and delight they're adding to the customer service experience?

American Express, ordinarily a terrific, data-driven marketer, has gone in almost entirely the wrong direction on this issue. Every letter and every phone call is designed to reduce costs, not to increase personal relationship and delight.

And with the amplifying power now available to many companies, on the web and off, will either us a weapon or be the victim of it.

Step By Step, Ideavirus Tactics

- Make it virusworthy.
  If it's not worth talking about, it won't get talked abc
- Identify the hive.
  You won't get the full benefit of the ideavirus until dominate your hive.
- Expose the idea.
  Expose it to the right people, and do whatever you nee to do to get those people deep into the experience of th idea as quickly as possible. Pay them if necessary, espe cially at the beginning. Never charge for exposure if you can help it.
- Figure out what you want the sneezers to say.
  You've got to decide what you want the sneezers to say to the population. If you don't decide, either they'll decide for you and say something less than optimal, or they won't even bother to spend the time.
- Give the sneezers the tools they need to spread the virus.
  After you've got a potential sneezer, make it easy for him to spread the idea. Give him a way to send your idea to someone else with one click. Let me join your affiliate program in sixty seconds or less. Reward the people I spread the virus to, so I don't feel guilty for spreading it.

Hudson River pollution problem—once a big factory is polluting the river, you might as well too.

Permission marketing, on the other hand, is self-limiting. When people have had enough, they'll stop giving permission to marketers, and thus there will be no clutter crisis. Sure, some folks will cheat by spamming or invading privacy or buying and selling names. But societal pressure and a few key government regulations should stop the cheaters.

But what about the ideavirus? After it dawns on marketers that it's working, won't we all be flooded by offers to make us promiscuous and an incredible flow of free this and free that?

You bet. I think a few things will occur:

1. The race goes to the swift. Just as Frank Zappa and David Bowie supercharged their careers by getting on CD early, some marketers will fill vacuums and enjoy profits for years to come. Latecomers will get hurt.

2. The cost of spreading a virus will increase. The bounties to turn people promiscuous will increase. The benefit to powerful sneezers will increase. When there's huge demand for recommendations, marketers will have to pay more to get them.

3. There will be a significant benefit to becoming a powerful sneezer. Everyone will want to be Esther Dyson or Walter Cronkite, because that sort of genuine credential can be turned into a profit for years and years. Thus, we'll see fewer institutional efforts and more individuals (free

agents) who figure out that they can profit mightily by spreading their own viruses (this manifesto is a living example of that technique).

4. It's going to be noisy and loud and cluttered as we transition, with a few huge winners and many satisfied marketers who dominate a hive but don't necessarily tip. After that, once the various media settle down, an equilibrium will return and (hopefully) the good stuff will win.

Good luck. Tell me how it goes for you!

Sethgodin@ideavirus.com

ACKNOWLEDGMENTS

First, some professional sneezing (you can find all these links at www.ideavirus.com as well):

1. If you ever get the chance to have Red Maxwell design something for you, grab it. He's an extraordinary talent, and even better, a brilliant project manager and a great friend. You can reach Red at red@designfactorynet.com.

2. One of the best ways to start and spread an ideavirus is to have your company write a book about it. Books are still the most leveraged way to get powerful sneezers to understand your ideas and spread them. And the partners at Lark Productions—Lisa DiMona, Karen Watts and Robin Dellabough (robinlark@mindspring.com) are among the best I've ever found at turning ideas into books.

3. If you haven't been reading *Fast Company,* don't panic. You can catch up on what you've missed at www.fastcompany.com. In a world of hype and shallowness, you'll find very little of either here.

4. Malcolm Gladwell's book, *The Tipping Point,* will radically shift your thinking. That's a good thing. Find this and his other writings at www.gladwell.com.

5. A lot of people haven't kept up with Tom Peters since they bought his very first book. Don't hesitate! I reread his stuff as often as I can. Find it at www.tompeters.com.

6. I also recommend four other great writers and thinkers. **Chris Meyer** co-wrote Blur among other things, and despite his protestations, is beginning to share my hairline. **Jay Levinson** is the original marketing bigthinker, and you're selling yourself short if you haven't picked up his books lately. And finally, **Don Peppers** and **Martha Rogers** who continue to be way ahead of me and everyone else in how they're deconstructing and reconstructing the way we think about marketing.

7. The guys at Peanut Press are terrific. If you've got a Palm, point your browser to www.peanutpress.com and go get some books for it. Thanks, Mike!

I'd also like to thank Susan Greenspan Cohen, Bob Dorf, Louise Wannier, Alison Heisler and the wonderful people at *Fast Company* (especially the incredible Alan Webber) for advice, insight and encouragement as I plowed through this manifesto. And thanks to my role model and friend Lester Wunderman.

Jerry Colonna, Fred Wilson, Bob Greene, Tom Cohen, Seth Goldstein and their friends, partners and associates at Flatiron Partners have been generous enough to give me a platform and a lab to mess with a lot of new thinking. They certainly keep me on my toes, and are nice enough to sit through my endless slide shows.* Steve Kane and Stu

---

* Fred Wilson and Tom Cohen, though, deserve extra thanks. Without the two of them, my internet company would have never thrived, and you wouldn't be reading this book.

Roseman are, amazingly enough, about to throw themselves into this maelstrom. Can't wait.

Thanks to Don Epstein and David Evenchick at the Greater Talent Network in New York City for believing in me and then being true to their word and keeping me busy.

For the last year, two people have done everything to keep things in perspective for me . . . Lisa Gansky and my Dad. Thanks, guys.

Of course, as always, the real joy in my life comes from my wife Helene and our little entrepreneurs, Alex and Max.

AFTERWORD

Do you remember the old days? The days when Procter & Gamble invaded our homes with ads for Wisk and there was a Marlboro Man billboard on every corner?

Those days have been waning for a while, but now they're officially over. Last week, Microsoft launched a major ad campaign. They hired the wise guys at the Modern Humorist (*www.modernhumorist.com*) to put together a campaign celebrating the death of that stupid little paper clip that shows up on the bottom of Microsoft Word. But don't take my word for it—you can see the clip get clipped at *www.officeclippy.com*.

While I'm as pleased as the next guy about the death of Clippy, I was stunned to see the form the campaign took. Rather than using television or newspapers or magazines or even web banners, Microsoft launched a viral campaign that depended on people telling their friends. It worked. The word spread. Amazingly, hundreds of people even posted notes on Slashdot, normally world headquarters for Microsoft-haters.

Viral marketing is spreading like . . . a virus. Procter & Gamble, home of the interruption ad, is now spending millions of dollars a year trying to identify and win over sneezers. The movie studios are deciding which films to make based on their potential to spread an ideavirus. And with campaign reform right around the corner, very senior people in Washington are working overtime trying to find something to replace those expensive (and increasingly ineffective) TV spots.

When this book was first published, the extent of the web meltdown was hardly known. The long Internet winter of 2001 was extraordinarily severe, so much so that many people decided to give up on the medium entirely. Not so fast. People haven't stopped using email. It's growing. Habits that were shaped during the go-go years are here to stay . . . the only thing that's new is that the valuations make a lot more sense. Marketing is going to be changed forever by the connections we've made online.

Smart ideavirus marketers are stepping into this media and money vacuum. They're discovering that the increasingly taut connections between people and the newfound power of the sneezer are exactly what they need to get the word out about their projects. New businesses, both online and off, are being built around the ideavirus concept.

Check out *www.helpafriend.com* for an example of how smart doctors are using the medium to help people get better fast. Or visit *www.norh.com* for a look at a totally different kind of hi-fi speaker company.

Doing It Right

When I first registered the domain ideavirus.com, a search on Google turned up exactly one match for the word "ideavirus." It seemed to be for an Icelandic fishing village, but I'm not sure, because the site was in Icelandic.

Within a week of posting the book online, more than 10,000 people had downloaded it. Today, as I look at Google again, I'm amazed to find more than 2,000 site matches—more than 2,000 sites on the web either hosting the book itself or writing about it. A 100,000 percent increase (from a very small base, of course) in less than a year.

I'll confess—I'm as amazed as the next guy.

Unleashing the Ideavirus was more than an ebook. It was an experiment in taking my own advice. By following the steps I outlined in this book, I set out to create a living, breathing example of how an ideavirus could be built and might spread.

So far, more than 250,000 people have downloaded the book directly from my site. Our research shows that the average person emails it to three friends. That means that more than a million copies are out there. Add to this the large number of sites (I have no idea how many) that are also making the book available for download and you've got the most downloaded ebook ever written.

I now want to address the question I get asked most often.

Why Give It Away?

The obvious question is this: "Business is not charity. How are you going to make any money if all you do is give stuff away?" This is not a dumb question.

I was lucky. I backed into doing it right because I tried very hard *not* to make money. If I were trying to make a profit from this project, this is what I would have done:

1. Put an expiration date on the download so that after a certain date you couldn't get it any longer.
2. Not allow other sites to offer the book for download.
3. Require people to give their email address and register in order to read the book.
4. Have paperback versions in the stores the day I announced the project.
5. Run ads in traditional and electronic media.

The reasons behind these tactics are related and perfectly natural. By limiting the download period, I could create an environment post-expiration where the only way to see the book would be to buy it. Surely this would sell more books. Same goes for not allowing other sites to offer it for download—by forcing people to my site, I'd keep control, gain eyeballs, and have great site statistics.

If I had registered everyone who downloaded the book, I'd have millions of email names, not just ten thousand. And if I'd had books in stores (and ads supporting them), I would have sold tons of books to people who chose not to read it online.

Fortunately, my goal was merely to experiment with the medium. My intentional avoidance of making income from this project is the main reason it succeeded so well!

Steps one through four in my list would have eliminated person-to-person pass-along of the ebook. If someone had to ask me every time they wanted to share it, or register if they wanted to read it, the amount of friction in the process would have grounded it to a halt. Instead of the average person sending the book to three or four friends, the number would have fallen to zero.

And what good would a million registrations have done if those million people didn't really want to hear from me? If someone registers for an email list they don't want in order to get something they *do* want, then the email that follows is unanticipated, impersonal, irrelevant junk. Instead of having a valuable asset of sneezers who were eager to get more information, I'd have a database of people waiting to flame me for spamming them every time I hit the send button.

There's no question in my mind that we would have sold far more books if the paper version had been ready at the same time as the e-version. But there's a silver lining here as well. Because there was no paper version, it made the ebook even more likely to spread. If there's a paper alternative, people will say, "That's okay, I'll read it in hard copy next week." (And of course, being lazy like me, they'll forget.) Without this alternative, many people forced themselves to sit through the always tedious download and on-screen reading process.

Of course, most people *didn't* finish the book online. Screens aren't made for reading, they're made for surfing and interacting, and for a long time to come, people are going to want to read books on paper. Three months later, when the book did come out (at a funky price point of $40—see the next section for more on that), there was a long line of people who had browsed the book and now wanted to read it.

So, for all the wrong financial reasons, I did everything I could to kill the sales of the book and increase its readership. The end result demonstrated a real truth about ideas: The more people who know your idea, the more your idea is worth.

With all these people reading the book, some funny things happened.

First, we sold a lot of copies in hardcover. The book went to number 5 on the Amazon bestseller list within forty-eight hours of being on sale. Second, we sold foreign rights to translations in almost a dozen countries (the Japanese version came out last month and promptly went to number 4 on Amazon Japan).

And, best of all, we put new words into the vocabulary of marketers everywhere. Words like sneezers and ideavirus and hive. Once people use your words, then your ideas are sure to follow.

In addition to book sales that far exceeded my expectations, I've been asked to give dozens of speeches around the world. Since those speeches are my primary livelihood, that's good news.

It hasn't been perfect. Not by any means. I did a lot of things wrong, some of them very wrong. But the lesson of giving up control and letting the market be in charge is the one I want to hammer home before I go through the mea culpas.

The market is right more than you are. The market also has more power than you do. More power to ignore you. More power to buy something else. Understanding that power, and more important, surrendering to that power is the way to get ahead of the competition.

Doing It Wrong, Part 1

I learned one valuable lesson from the success of the ebook. People are not as price sensitive as most people think, but they are more price sensitive than I thought.

To make a point about the value of souvenirs, I intentionally set the price point for the hardcover at $40. I figured that a $40 price point would separate the people looking for the idea (which they could get for free) from those wanting a souvenir edition (which is printed on paper).

On one hand, this price point probably maximized our short-term profits. But in the long run, it was dumb. Forty dollars was too much for this book, hence the paperback you hold in your hands. While many people were happy to pay $40 for the souvenir edition (bought on the company credit card!), many people hesitated. Now they were stuck with reading it online (which they didn't want to do because it's hard to read online or because they had technical issues) or buying a different book on the topic.

Lesson: Even after your idea spreads, keeping your price point as reasonable as you can is just plain smart.

Doing It Wrong, Part 2

Taking what I'd learned, I needed to figure out what to do with my next book. It's not really a book, actually, it's more of a booklet. A 98-page booklet about how to design websites that work better.

I was tempted to follow in the footsteps of the ideavirus and just give it away. After all, I knew that would work. But always looking for something new, I called up Amazon and asked if they had a use for it.

It turns out that Amazon was about to launch an ebook store and wanted to feature my new book, *The Big Red Fez*, in the launch. We set the lowest price point they would allow ($3), and I decided to give my huge royalties (thirty cents a copy!) to the Juvenile Diabetes Foundation.

The book was encrypted in Adobe eBook Reader format, which is brand new. They put up the site and we all admired it.

The next day, I did a mailing to my core group of sneezers.

So far, so good. I had a product I was proud of. I knew the hive, and I had permission from the sneezers. I sent them a note that made getting the book fast and easy. And then, over the Easter weekend, we watched.

The first response was terrific. Within a day, it was the bestselling ebook on Amazon, perhaps the fastest-selling ebook in their history. People *were* willing to pay for an ebook if it was fresh and new and on a topic they trusted. (Didn't hurt, either, that the only place in the world to get the book was online.)

Then we hit the fan. The first problem was that due to a snafu at Amazon, the Macintosh version of eBook Reader wasn't readily available. Worse, most users didn't figure this out until *after* they'd paid for and downloaded the book. I lost a bunch of sneezers right there.

Second, a few people had trouble printing the book out. The fact is that digital rights management (DRM) is in its very early stages, and no one really has a software solution that is both supereasy to use and hacker-proof.

More than a million people downloaded *Unleashing the Ideavirus* and I got a total of fourteen email complaints. After just a few days of marketing *The Big Red Fez*, I got three times that number.

But the real mistake was this—sales for the book leveled off fast. There was no second or third order bump due to word of mouse. Because it was hard to share, people didn't share. It wasn't smooth. It wasn't viral. It didn't spread.

This medium is very powerful, but it's also very picky. Before each and every referral, the reader/user/prospect faces a choice. If the user decides not to spread the word, the word doesn't spread. Whatever it is has to be so exceptional and so smooth that the user wants to take the risk of spreading the word to a trusted friend.

By the time you hold this book in your hand, it's likely that *The Big Red Fez* will be available for free. If you'd like a copy as thanks for reading all the way to the end of this book, stop by *www.thebigredfez.com* and I'll tell you where to get it. If it's not free, I'll tell you why not.

Thanks for reading.

INDEX

Index

Index

Index